The Yearbook of Comfort and Joy

Now may this little book a blessing be
To those that love this little book and me;
And may its buyer have no cause to say
His money is but lost or thrown away.

JOHN BUNYAN

Also by Celia Haddon
published by Michael Joseph

A BOOK OF FRIENDS AND FRIENDSHIP
A CHRISTMAS POSY
A LOVER'S POSY
A MOTHER'S POSY
THE POWER OF LOVE
GIFTS FROM YOUR GARDEN
THE YEARBOOK OF HOPE AND INSPIRATION
THE YEARBOOK OF COURAGE AND SERENITY
LOVELY IS THE ROSE
THE YEARBOOK OF LOVE AND WISDOM

CELIA HADDON

The Yearbook of Comfort and Joy

MICHAEL JOSEPH

LONDON

To
Caz McAree

MICHAEL JOSEPH LTD

Published by the Penguin Group
27 Wrights Lane, London W8 5TZ, England
Viking Penguin Inc., 375 Hudson Street, New York, New York 10014, USA
Penguin Books Canada Ltd, 10 Alcorn Avenue, Toronto, Ontario, Canada M4V 3B2
Penguin Books (NZ) Ltd, 182–190 Wairau Road, Auckland 10, New Zealand

Penguin Books Ltd Registered Offices: Harmondsworth, Middlesex, England

9

Design and computer page make-up
Penny Mills

Colour origination by Anglia Graphics, Bedford
Printed and bound by Kyodo in Singapore

A CIP catalogue record for this book is available from the
British Library

ISBN 0 7181 3422 2

Library of Congress Catalog Card Number: 91- 61159

This book grew out of my own great need for comfort and joy. In the autumn of 1988 I fell into great unhappiness. I felt I had no right to go on living. To help myself, I started a collection of quotations to comfort me and to see me through the pain. I needed to remind myself that life was worth living, that I myself deserved to live it and that my inner pain had some purpose and some meaning, even if I could not see what this was.

During the painful months of recovery there were moments of strangely intense joy – in the beauty of ordinary things, joy in a feeling that I had the right to be alive, joy in accepting myself with all my faults and joy in a realization that my pain was not wasted. I have survived. Looking back a year later, I am glad I was forced on to this road from despair towards inner peace. I have not arrived: I am still journeying.

Many of the writers I have quoted passed the same way. By sharing them with you, I hope to pass on the comfort they gave me. I have illustrated this book with the oil paintings of my mother, the painter Joyce Haddon; they help me see joy around me. Other illustrations come from my own collection of Victorian children's books and cards.

Celia Haddon

JANUARY

JANUARY 1

For the beginning of a new year, and a new book, I shall borrow words from the seventeenth-century mystic, Thomas Traherne

An empty book is like an infant's soul, in which anything may be written. I have a mind to fill this with profitable wonders. I will fill it with those truths you love without knowing them; and with those things which, if it be possible, shall shew my love to you, in communicating most enriching truths. As iron at a distance is drawn by the loadstone, there being some invisible communications between them, so is there in us a world of love to somewhat, though we know not what in the world that should be. There are invisible ways of conveyance by which some great thing doth touch our souls, and by which we tend to it.

JANUARY 2

The infinite shining heavens
Rose and I saw in the night
Uncountable angel stars
Showering sorrow and light.

Night after night in my sorrow
The stars stood over the sea,
Till lo! I looked in the dusk
And a star had come down to me.

ROBERT LOUIS STEVENSON

JANUARY 3

A hard icy frost can transform ordinary surroundings into glittering new world – as Ambrose Philips's poem describes. Let me not ignore the radiant splendour of ice and snow and frost.

For every shrub, and every blade of grass,
And every pointed thorn, seemed wrought in glass.
In pearls and rubies rich the hawthorns show,
While through the ice the crimson berries glow.
The thick-sprung reeds the watery marshes yield,
Seem polished lances in a hostile field.
The stag in limpid currents with surprise
Sees crystal branches on his forehead rise.
The spreading oak, the beech, and towering pine,
Glazed over, in the freezing aether shine.
When if a sudden gust of wind arise,
The brittle forest into atoms flies:
The crackling wood beneath the tempest bends,
And in a spangled shower the prospect ends.

JANUARY 4

Joy exists only in self acceptance. Seek perfect acceptance, not a perfect life.

AUTHOR UNKNOWN

JANUARY 5

Our fireside's easy chair –
Is there any place beside
Can such pleasant cheer prepare
As our own fireside?
Though humble be the fare,
That want's daily toils provide,
Dainty's pomp can ne'er compare
With the joy want meeteth there
By his own fireside.

JOHN CLARE

JANUARY 6

Love has a hundred gentle ends.

LEONORA SPEYER

JANUARY 7

Ask you who is singing here
Who so blithe can thus appear?
I'm the child of joy and glee,
And my name's Variety.

I do not know who wrote this, but I know that what it says is very true. Sometimes the cure for depression or persistent anxiety is to divert the mind by a change and take time away from problems.

JANUARY 8

Look backward with gratitude.
Look onward with hope.
Look upward with confidence.

My friends, Alan and Mollie Posner, sent me a card with this message. When I can do this, troubles no longer trouble me.

JANUARY 9

God doth not need
Either man's work or his own gifts: who best
Bear his mild yoke, they serve him best; His state
Is kingly; thousands at His bidding speed,
And post o'er land and ocean without rest;
They also serve who only stand and wait.

JOHN MILTON

JANUARY 10

It takes seventy-two muscles to frown, but only thirteen to smile.

This reminder came from a newsletter sent to traffic wardens. Sometimes using those thirteen muscles makes my whole mood alter – putting on a smile can lift my heart on an otherwise gloomy day.

JANUARY 11

A little health,
A little wealth,
A little house and freedom,
And at the end
A little friend
And little cause to need him.

This recipe for the good life comes from a Victorian sampler.

JANUARY 12

Knowledge is the antidote to fear – knowledge, use and reason. Knowledge is the encourager, knowledge that takes fear out of the heart, knowledge and use, which is knowledge in practice. They can conquer who believe they can.

RALPH WALDO EMERSON

JANUARY 13

A merry tale with a friend refresheth a man much, and without any harm lighteth his mind and amendeth his courage; so that it seemeth but well done to take such recreation. And St Thomas saith that proper pleasant talking is a good virtue, serving to refresh the mind and make it quick and lusty to study again, where continual fatigation would make it dull and deadly.

SIR THOMAS MORE

JANUARY 14

I love this tender little verse by Francis Quarles and its message is one I need to remember when I feel God is far away.

E'en as a nurse, whose child's imperfect pace
Can hardly lead his foot from place to place,
Leaves her fond kissing, sets him down to go,
Nor does uphold him for a step or two;
But when she finds that he begins to fall
She holds him up, and kisses him withal: –
So God from man sometimes withdraws His hand
Awhile, to teach his infant faith to stand;
But when He sees his feeble strength begin
To fail, He gently takes him up again.

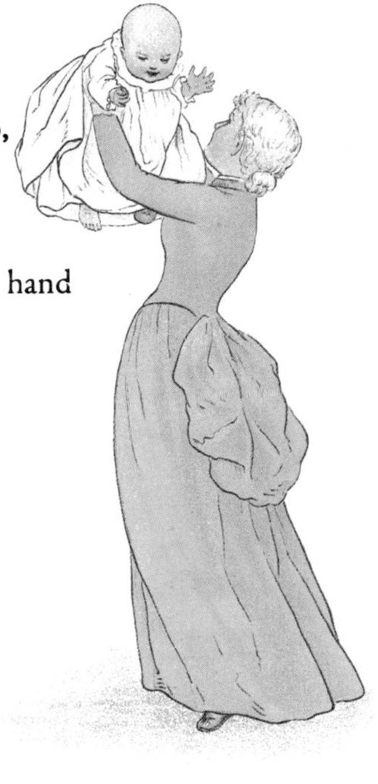

JANUARY 15

Sometimes outcasts have a vision denied to the comfortable and well-off. Francis Thompson, a failed priest and an opium addict, had a great sense of God. This poem is addressed to a snowflake.

What heart could have thought you? –
Past our devisal
(O filigree petal!)
Fashioned so purely,
Fragilely, surely.
From what Paradisal
Imagineless metal,
Too costly for cost?
Who hammered you, wrought you,
From argentine vapour? –
'God was my shaper,
Passing surmisal,
He hammered me, He wrought me.'

JANUARY 16

Joy is prayer; joy is strength; joy is love; joy is a net of love by which you can catch souls. A joyful heart is the inevitable result of a heart burning with love.

MOTHER TERESA
OF CALCUTTA

JANUARY 17

May joy and ease, and affluence and content,
And the light conscience of a life well spent,
Calm every thought, inspirit every grace,
Glow in thy heart, smile upon thy face.

ALEXANDER POPE

JANUARY 18

Through not observing what is in the mind of another, a man has seldom been seen to be unhappy. But those who do not observe the movements of their own mind must of necessity be unhappy.

Marcus Aurelius's words remind me that to be happy I need to focus on myself not on the feelings or doings of others. This is the way to care for myself and improve myself.

JANUARY 19

My dog, the trustiest of his kind,
With gratitude inflames my mind;
I mark his true, his faithful way,
And in my service copy Tray.

John Gay's poem about his dog, Tray, says something which has struck most dog lovers – their trust, their fidelity and the love they give us, cast our own doubtful characters into the shade.

JANUARY 20

I am not bound to win, but I am bound to be true. I am not bound to succeed, but I am bound to live up to what light I have. I must stand with anybody that stands right; stand with him while he is right, and part with him when he goes wrong.

ABRAHAM LINCOLN

JANUARY 21

To love oneself in the right way and to love one's neighbour are at bottom one and the same. When selfishness has been taken from you, then you have learned to love yourself rightly. When a man in self torment thinks to do God a service by torturing himself, what is his sin except this, of not willing to love himself in the right way?

SOREN KIERKEGAARD

JANUARY 22

Change frightens me, yet often change is necessary. James Russell Lowell's verse helps me accept change which must come.

Come out, then, from the old thoughts and old ways,
Before you harden to a crystal cold
Which the new life can shatter, but not mould:
Freedom for you still waits, still, looking backward,
 stays,
But widens still the irretrievable space.

JANUARY 23

Take short views, hope for the best, and trust in God.

SYDNEY SMITH

JANUARY 24

We see but dimly through the mists and vapours;
Amid these earthly damps,
What seem to us but sad, funereal tapers
May be heaven's distant lamps.

HENRY WADSWORTH LONGFELLOW

JANUARY 25

Robert Burns, the great Scottish poet born today, knew that the secret of a good life is to try to be contented, to take life as it comes rather than make demands upon it. Tonight is Burns night.

Life is but a day at most,
Sprung from night, in darkness lost;
Hope not sunshine every hour,
Fear not clouds will always lour.
Happiness is but a name,
Make content and ease thy aim.

JANUARY 26

The heart of man has been so constituted by the Almighty, that like a flint, it contains a hidden fire which is evoked by music and harmony, and renders man beside himself with ecstasy. These harmonies are echoes of that higher world of beauty which we call the world of spirits; they remind man of his relationship to that world, and produce in him an emotion so deep and strange that he himself is powerless to explain it.

Al-Ghazzali, the author of these words about music, was an Islamic mystic. I need reminding of the power of music to calm and comfort me with its harmony. I must make time to listen.

JANUARY 27

When I am very worried about something, I often find I cannot get my difficulties into perspective. I have found this story about the founder of Methodism, John Wesley, helpful. He was walking one day with a friend, who confided to him that he was in great trouble and didn't know where to turn. As they walked they passed a stone wall over which a cow was looking. John Wesley said:

Do you know why that cow looks over that wall? I will tell you. She looks over the wall because she cannot see through it, and that is what you must do with your troubles – look over and *above* them.

JANUARY 28

O Lady! we receive but what we give,
And in our life alone does nature live:
Ours is her wedding garment, ours her shroud!
And would we aught behold, of higher worth,
Than that inanimate cold world allowed
To the poor loveless ever-anxious crowd,
Ah! from the soul itself must issue forth
A light, a glory, a fair luminous cloud
Enveloping the earth.

SAMUEL TAYLOR COLERIDGE

JANUARY 29

A new life begins for us with every second. Let us go forward joyously to meet it. We must press on, whether we will or no, and we shall walk better with our eyes before us than with them ever cast behind.

JEROME K. JEROME

JANUARY 30

To laugh is to risk appearing a fool.
To weep is to risk appearing sentimental.
To reach out for another is to risk involvement.
To reveal your feelings is to risk exposing your true self.
To place your ideas and dreams before the crowd is to risk
their loss.
To love is to risk not being loved in return.
To hope is to risk disappointment.
But risks must be taken because the greatest risk in life is to
risk nothing.
The person who risks nothing, does nothing, sees nothing,
has nothing and is nothing.
He cannot learn, feel, change, grow, love and live.
Chained by his certitude he is a slave.
He has forfeited his freedom.
Only a person who risks is free.

AUTHOR UNKNOWN

JANUARY 31

And well the tiny things of earth
Repay the watching eye.

EBENEZER ELLIOTT

FEBRUARY

FEBRUARY 1

Let your mind be quiet, realizing the beauty of the world,
and the immense, the boundless treasures that it
holds in store.
All that you have within you, all that your heart
desires, all that your nature so specially fits you for –
that or the counterpart of it waits embedded in the
great Whole, for you. It will surely come to you.
Yet equally surely not one moment before its appointed
time will it come. All your crying and fever and
reaching out of hands will make no difference.
Therefore do not begin that game at all.

EDWARD CARPENTER

FEBRUARY 2

Sometimes I go into churches to sit a little while in their calm. I am not a Catholic but I often light a candle. Last time I was doing this, I came across a leaflet with these lines. Today is Candlemas, a day for candles, so I shall share them with you.

Lighting a candle is a sign of our prayer for someone and the offering of our lives; a reminder to us and others of the men and women who have shone as lights of the world; a witness to all who pass by that this is a place of prayer. To find the words to pray is difficult and we do not know what to say for the best. Our hearts are too full for words. Our anxieties paralyse us. Light a candle. Let the spirit of God work in you and let it lead you in prayer.

FEBRUARY 3

One way I fight off unhappiness is to learn something new. Applying the mind, whether it is learning a new needlework stitch, a new language or studying algebra, takes its focus away from our troubles. I found the idea in a letter written by Sir Philip Sidney, the great Elizabethan poet, statesman and courtier.

I am often more serious than either my age or my pursuits demand; yet this I have learned by experience, that I am never less a prey to melancholy than when I am earnestly applying the feeble powers of my mind to some high and difficult object.

FEBRUARY 4

Set here to grow, what should we do
But take what soil and climate give?
For thence must come out sap and hue.
The future let us not permit
To choke us in its shadow's clasp;
It cannot touch us, nor we it;
The present moment's in our grasp.

These lines by William Allingham tell us to live in the present, accept it fully, and to cast out any anxieties about the future.

FEBRUARY 5

Strew human life with flowers; save every hour for the sunshine; exalt your souls; widen the sympathies of your heart; make joy real now to those you love, and help forward the joy of those yet to be born.

RICHARD JEFFERIES

FEBRUARY 6

Be near me when my light is low,
When the blood creeps, and the nerves prick
And tingle; and the heart is sick
And all the wheels of being slow.

Be near me when the sensuous frame
Is racked with pangs that conquer trust;
And Time, a maniac scattering dust,
And Life, a fury slinging flame.

ALFRED, LORD TENNYSON

FEBRUARY 7

Out of evil, much good has come to me. By keeping quiet, remaining attentive, and, hand in hand with that, by accepting reality – taking things as they are, and not as I wanted them to be – by doing all this, rare knowledge has come to me, and rare powers as well. I always thought that, when we accept things, they overpower us in one way or another. Now I intend being receptive to whatever comes to me, good and bad, sun and shadow, and, in this way, also accepting my own nature with its positive and negative sides.

A PATIENT'S LETTER TO ERNEST JUNG

FEBRUARY 8

Friendship is the inexpressible comfort of feeling safe with a person, having neither to weigh thoughts nor measure words.

JEREMY TAYLOR

FEBRUARY 9

Who has not found the heaven below,
Will fail of it above:
For angels rent the house next our's
Wherever we remove.

EMILY DICKINSON

FEBRUARY 10

If you want to raise a man from mud and filth, do not think it is enough to keep standing on top and reaching down to him a helping hand. You must go all the way down yourself, down into the mud and filth. Then take hold of him with strong hands and pull him and yourself out into the light.

RABBI SHELOMO

FEBRUARY 11

Sweet are the thoughts that savour of content:
The quiet mind is richer than a crown.
Sweet are the nights in careless slumber spent;
The poor estate scorns fortune's angry frown.
Such sweet content, such minds, such sleep, such bliss
Beggars enjoy when princes oft do miss.

The art of contentment is rarely cultivated in the modern world. Yet it remains the way to happiness, says the poet Robert Greene.

FEBRUARY 12

When the ground was partially bare of snow, and a few warm days had dried its surface somewhat, it was pleasant to compare the first tender signs of the infant year just peering forth with the stately beauty of the withered vegetation which had withstood the winter. The first sparrow of spring! The year beginning with younger hope than ever! What at such times are histories, chronologies, traditions and all written revelations!

Henry David Thoreau, the American philosopher who went to live in a log cabin in the woods for two years, found his inspiration in nature. We can too. Even from a city flat we can hear the chirps of the mating sparrows and see the first bulbs in the park. It is time to take fresh hope for the coming spring.

FEBRUARY 13

For snowdrops are the harbinger of spring,
A sort of link between dumb life and light,
Freshness preserved amid all withering,
Bloom in the midst of grey and frostly blight,
Pale stars that gladden Nature's dreary night.

CAROLINE NORTON

FEBRUARY 14

This poem was written by the American Anne Bradstreet to her husband three centuries ago. It is one of the few poems that celebrate the joys of long-lasting love, so I dedicate it here to my own partner, Ronnie, and to any couple in a long-lasting, friendly, comfortable and loving relationship, for Valentine's day.

If ever two were one, then surely we.
If ever man were loved by wife, then thee:
If ever wife was happy in a man,
Compare with me ye women if you can.
I prize thy love more than whole mines of gold,
Or all the riches that the East doth hold.
My love is such that rivers cannot quench,
Nor aught but love from thee, give recompense.
Thy love is such I can no way repay,
The heavens reward thee manifold I pray.
Then while we live, in love let's so persever,
That when we live no more, we may live ever.

FEBRUARY 15

The affirmative of affirmatives is love.

RALPH WALDO EMERSON

FEBRUARY 16

Home's home, although it reached be
Through wet and dirt and night; though heartily
I welcomed was, yet something still
Methinks was wanting to fulfil
Content's odd appetite; no cheer,
Say I, so good as that which meets me here.

JOSEPH BEAUMONT

FEBRUARY 17

Almighty Father, Thy love is like a great sea that girdles the earth. Out of the deep we come to float awhile upon its surface. We cannot sound its depth nor tell its greatness, only we know it never faileth. The winds that blow over us are the breathing of Thy spirit; the sun that lights and warms us is Thy truth. Now Thou does suffer us to sail calm seas; now Thou dost buffet us with storms of trouble; on the crest of waves of sorrow Thou dost raise us, but it is Thy love that bears us up; in the trough of desolation Thou dost sink us, that we may see nought but Thy love on every side. And when we pass into the deep again, the waters of Thy love encompass and enfold us.

ANONYMOUS

FEBRUARY 18

Let praise devote thy work, and skill employ
Thy whole mind, and thy heart be lost in joy.
For God requires no more than thou hast done,
And takes thy work to bless it for His own.

ROBERT BRIDGES

FEBRUARY 19

In the infinite universe there is room for our swiftest diligence and to spare. Even in a corner of it, in a private park, or in the neighbourhood of a single hamlet, the weather and the seasons keep so deftly changing that although we walk there for a lifetime there will be always something new to startle and delight us.

ROBERT LOUIS STEVENSON

FEBRUARY 20

Blessed are the poor in spirit, for theirs is the kingdom
of heaven.
Blessed are they that mourn, for they shall be comforted.
Blessed are the meek, for they shall inherit the earth.
Blessed are they which do hunger and thirst
after righteousness, for they shall be filled.
Blessed are the merciful, for they shall obtain mercy.
Blessed are the pure in heart for they shall see God.
Blessed are the peacemakers, for they shall be called
the children of God.

The young Jewish teacher Jesus from Nazareth who spoke these words two thousand years ago came with a message of love, and forgiveness for the outcast, the poor and the troubled in mind.

FEBRUARY 21

Happiness is as a butterfly which, when pursued, is always beyond our grasp, but which, if you will sit down quietly, may alight upon you.

Happiness can't be snatched. It has to come naturally, as part of a life well lived, says the American writer, Nathaniel Hawthorne.

FEBRUARY 22

To the good I act with goodness; to the bad I also act with goodness: thus goodness is attained. To the faithful I act with faith; to the faithless I also act with faith: thus faith is attained.

These words by the Chinese sage, Lao Tzu, come from a Bhuddist book called the Tao Te Ching, *written well before the birth of Christ.*

FEBRUARY 23

'I have no name:
I am but two days old.'
What shall I call thee?
'I happy am,
Joy is my name.'
Sweet joy befall thee
Pretty joy!
Sweet joy but two days old,
Sweet joy I call thee:
Thou dost smile,
I sing the while,
Sweet joy befall thee.

WILLIAM BLAKE

FEBRUARY 24

Long as there's a sun that sets,
Primroses will have their glory;
Long as there are violets,
They will have a place in story:
There's a flower that shall be mine
'Tis the little celandine.

Comfort have thou of thy merit,
Kindly, unassuming spirit!
Careless of thy neighbourhood,
Thou dost show thy pleasant face
On the moor, and in the wood,
In the lane; – there's not a place
Howsoever mean it be,
But 'tis good enough for thee.

WILLIAM WORDSWORTH

FEBRUARY 25

A fallen soufflé is just a risen omelette. It depends on how you look at it, that's all – from above or below.

RABBI LIONEL BLUE

FEBRUARY 26

'O dreary life,' we cry, 'O dreary life!'
And still the generations of the birds
Sing through our sighing, and the flocks and herds
Serenely live while we are keeping strife
With Heaven's true purpose in us...
O thou God of old,
Grant me some smaller grace than comes to these! –
But so much patience as a blade of grass
Grows by, contented through the heat and cold.

ELIZABETH BARRETT BROWNING

FEBRUARY 27

Now may every living thing, young or old, weak or strong, living near or far, known or unknown, living or departed or yet unborn, may every living thing be full of bliss.

THE BUDDHA

FEBRUARY 28

Let your trouble be,
Light will follow dark:
Though the heaven falls,
You may hear the lark.

JOHANN GOETHE

FEBRUARY 29

Time flies, suns rise, and shadows fall –
Let them go by, for love is over all.

This little couplet comes from a sundial. It seems the right sentiment for a day on which women may propose marriage.

MARCH

MARCH 1

To mark St David's day, patron saint of Wales, there is this lovely Celtic benediction. I heard it first used in an open-air service in the Somerset countryside. It seemed to offer me both the peace and the encouragement which I needed and still need in difficult times. I find it hard to feel a sense of peace. This helps.

Deep peace of the running wave to you.
Deep peace of the flowing air to you.
Deep peace of the quiet earth to you.
Deep peace of the shining stars to you.
Deep peace of the Son of Peace to you.

MARCH 2

It may indeed be fantasy when I
Essay to draw from all created things
Deep, heartfelt, inward joy that closely clings;
And trace in leaves and flowers that round me lie
Lessons of love and earnest piety.
So let it be; and if the wide world rings
In mock of this belief, it brings
Nor fear, nor grief, nor vain perplexity.
So will I build my altar in the fields,
And the blue sky my fretted dome shall be,
And the sweet fragrance that the wild flower yields
Shall be the incense I will yield to Thee,
The only God!

SAMUEL TAYLOR COLERIDGE

MARCH 3

I believe that a leaf of grass is no less than the
journey-work of the stars,
And the pismire is equally perfect, and a grain of sand,
and the egg of the wren,
And the tree-toad is a *chef d'oeuvre* for the highest,
And the running blackberry would adorn the parlours of
heaven,
And the narrowest hinge in my hand puts to scorn all
machinery,
And the cow crunching with depressed head surpasses
any statue,
And a mouse is miracle enough to stagger sextillions of
infidels.

WALT WHITMAN

MARCH 4

Poetry is the record of the best and happiest moments of the happiest and best minds. Poetry makes immortal all that is best and most beautiful in the world. Poetry redeems from decay the visitations of the divinity in man.

One of the joys we can share is poetry, says the poet Percy Bysshe Shelley. It helps us see the divinity within ourselves.

MARCH 5

All we are asked to bear we can bear. That is a law of the spiritual life. The only hindrance to the working of this law, as of all benign laws, is fear.

ELIZABETH GOUDGE

MARCH 6

The old almanacks said that today was the first day of spring. It is a time when birds, even in cities, start singing in the morning. Their song, says Richard Jefferies, can help us start the day well.

It is sweet on awaking in the early morn to listen to the small bird singing on the tree. All that is delicious and beloved of spring time are expressed in his song. Nor is it necessary it should be a song; a few short notes in the morning are sufficient to stir the heart.

MARCH 7

What then? Shall we sit idly down and say
The night hath come; it is no longer day?
Something remains for us to do or dare;
Even the oldest tree some fruit may bear;
For age is opportunity no less
Than youth itself, though in another dress,
And as the evening twilight fades away
The sky is filled with stars invisible by day.

HENRY WADSWORTH LONGFELLOW

MARCH 8

I am an old man and have had many troubles, but most of them never happened.

A Victorian inscription found carved over a mantelpiece.

MARCH 9

O Earth! thou hast not any wind that blows
Which is not music; every weed of thine
Pressed rightly flows in aromatic wine;
And every humble hedgerow flower that grows,
And every little brown bird that doth sing,
Hath something greater than itself, and bears
A living word to every living thing,
Albeit it hold the message unawares.

RICHARD REALF

MARCH 10

Friendship with oneself is all important because without it one cannot be friends with anyone else in the world.

These words by Eleanor Roosevelt help me when I cannot love myself and I feel trapped by self hatred and self doubt.

MARCH 11

It fortifies my soul to know
That though I perish, Truth is so:
That, howso'er I stray and range,
Whate'er I do, Thou dost not change.
I steadier step when I recall
That, if I slip, Thou dost not fall.

There's something reassuring about this verse by Arthur Hugh Clough. I feel that in bad times it helps me keep plodding onward.

MARCH 12

Know yourself, love yourself, give of yourself.

This was read out at a funeral. I do not know where it comes from but it sums up, for me, what I may achieve by the end of my life.

MARCH 13

Lord, purge our eyes to see
Within the seed a tree,
Within the glowing egg a bird,
Within the shroud a butterfly:

Till taught by such, we see
Beyond all creatures Thee,
And hearken for Thy tender word,
And hear it, 'Fear not: it is I.'

CHRISTINA ROSSETTI

MARCH 14

No receipt openeth the heart but a true friend, to whom you may impart griefs, joys, hopes, suspicions, counsels and whatsoever lieth upon the heart to oppress it. This communicating of a man's self to his friend works two contrary effects, for it redoubleth joys and cutteth grief in halves. For there is no man that imparteth his joys to his friends but he joyeth the more, and no man that imparteth his griefs to his friend but he grieveth the less.

SIR FRANCIS BACON

MARCH 15 *At times of exhaustion and stress, there is comfort to be found in the animals about us. They don't complain. The patient humility of donkeys inspired this verse by the French poet, Francis Jammes.*

Let me appear before you among these beasts,
That I so love because they softly bow their heads,
And, as they stand, they join their little hooves
With humble gentleness that makes you pity them.
And, as I lie by your heavenly waters,
In this sojourn of the soul,
Let me be like the donkeys,
Whose sweet and humble poverty
Is clearly mirrored in the eternal love.

MARCH 16 I saw a delicate flower had grown up two feet high, between the horses' path and the wheel-track. An inch more to the right or left had sealed its fate, or an inch higher; and yet it lived to flourish as much as if it had a thousand acres of untrodden space around it, and never knew the danger it occurred. It did not borrow trouble, nor invite an evil fate by apprehending it.

HENRY DAVID THOREAU

For St Patrick's Day, some lines by the saint himself. MARCH 17

May the strength of God pilot us.
May the power of God preserve us.
May the wisdom of God instruct us.
May the hand of God protect us.
May the way of God direct us.

The Victorian writer John Ruskin urged his readers to exercise the talent of curiosity. To discover and learn is to live more fully. MARCH 18

Curiosity is a gift, a capacity of pleasure in knowing, which if you destroy, you make yourselves cold and dull.

MARCH 19

Since health our toil rewards,
And strength is labour's prize,
I hate not, nor despise
The work my lot accords;
Nor fret with fears unkind
The tender joys, that bless
My hard-won peace of mind
In hours of idleness.

ROBERT BRIDGES

These lines were found scrawled on a cellar wall in Cologne, the German city that was destroyed by bombing in the last world war. MARCH 20

I believe in the sun, even when it is not shining. I believe in love, even when I do not feel it. I believe in God, even when He is silent.

MARCH 21 Our continual mistake is that we do not concentrate upon the present day, the actual hour, of our life: we live in the past or in the future; we are continually expecting the coming of some special moment when our life will unfold itself in its full significance. And we do not notice that life is flowing like water through our fingers.

FATHER ALEXANDER ELCHANINOV

MARCH 22

Where'er the gentle heart
Finds courage from above;
Where'er the heart forsook
Warms with the breath of love;
Where faith bids fear depart,
City of God! thou art.

FRANCIS TURNER PALGRAVE

MARCH 23 While you are upon earth, enjoy the good things that are here (to that end were they given), and be not melancholy, and wish yourself in heaven.

JOHN SELDEN

MARCH 24 They that sow in tears, shall reap in joy. He that now goeth forth and weepeth, bearing precious seed, shall doubtless come again with rejoicing, bringing his sheaves with him.

As Psalm 126 says, sorrow will eventually change to joy. A motto for both emotions is: 'This too shall pass.'

MARCH 25

In everyone there is something precious, which is in no one else. That is why it is said: 'Despise not any man.'

RABBI PINHAS

MARCH 26

And mark the flowers around us, how they live
Not for themselves, as we may feel,
But the delight which they to others give.
For nature never will her gifts conceal
From those who love to seek them – here amid
These trees how many doth disclose their pride,
From the unthinking rustic only hid
Who never turns him from the road aside
To look for beauties which he heedeth not.
It give us greater zest to feel the joys
We meet in this sweet solemn-suited spot
And with high ecstasies one's mind employs
To bear the worst that fickle life prepares,
Finding her sweets as common as her cares.

JOHN CLARE

MARCH 27

And when, upon some showery day,
Into a path or public way
A frog leaps out from bordering grass,
Startling the timid as they pass,
Do you observe him, and endeavour
To take the intruder into favour;
Learning from him to find a reason
For a light heart in a dull season?

I love these lines written by Dorothy Wordsworth, sister of the poet William. All of us need to find a light heart in a dull season.

MARCH 28

To do anything, to dig a hole in the ground, to plant a cabbage, to hit a mark, to move a shuttle, to work a pattern – in a word, to attempt to produce any effect and to succeed, has something in it that carries off the restless activity of the mind of man. Indolence is a delightful but distressing state; we must be doing something to be happy.

The essayist William Hazlitt here perceives an interesting truth. Activity calms the mind. Some people, whose fatigue is boredom, need activity not rest.

MARCH 29

One Spirit – his
Who wore the plaited thorns with bleeding brows –
Rules universal nature. Not a flower
But shows some touch, in freckle, streak or stain,
Of his unrivalled pencil. He inspires
Their balmy odours, and imparts their hues,
And bathes their eyes with nectar, and includes,
In grains as countless as the seaside sands,
The forms with which he sprinkles all the earth.

WILLIAM COWPER

MARCH 30

Where you do not find love, put love – and then you will find love.

ST JOHN OF THE CROSS

MARCH 31

As if the cares of human life were few
We seek out new,
And follow fate which would too fast pursue.
See how on every bough the birds express
In their sweet notes their happiness.
They all enjoy and nothing spare,
But on their mother Nature lay their care:
Why then should man, the lord of all below,
Such troubles choose to know
As none of all his subjects undergo?

JOHN DRYDEN

APRIL

The compliments of the season to my worthy masters and a merry first of April to us all! Beshrew the man who on such a day as this, the general festival, should affect to stand aloof. I love a Fool – as naturally as if I were of kith and kin to him. I have never made an acquaintance that lasted: or a friendship that answered; with any that had not some tincture of the absurd in their characters. The more laughable blunders a man shall commit in your company, the more tests he giveth you, that he will not betray or overreach you. And take my word for this, reader, and say a fool told it you, if you please, that he who hath not a dram of folly in his mixture, hath pounds of much worse matter in his composition. APRIL 1

Charles Lamb's well-known essay on All Fools' Day reminds us that there are worse faults than foolishness and that perhaps it is not wise to be wise all the time. A little playing the fool cheers us.

Now each creature joys the other APRIL 2
Passing happy days and hours:
One bird reports unto another
By the fall of silver showers;
Whilst the earth, our common mother,
Hath her bosom decked with flowers.

SAMUEL DANIEL

APRIL 3

Now dance the lights on lawn and lea,
The flocks are whiter down the vale,
And milkier every milky sail
On winding stream or distant sea;

Where now the seamew pipes, or dives
In yonder greening gleam, and fly
The happy birds, that change their sky
To build and brood; that live their lives

From land to land; and in my breast
Spring wakens too; and my regret
Becomes an April violet,
And buds and blossoms like the rest.

ALFRED, LORD TENNYSON

APRIL 4

Prayer is the peace of our spirit, the stillness of our thoughts, the evenness of our recollection, the seat of meditation, the rest of our cares and the calm of our tempest. Prayer is the issue of a quiet mind, of untroubled thoughts.

JEREMY TAYLOR

APRIL 5

Smile at each other; smile at your wife, smile at your husband, smile at your children, smile at each other – it doesn't matter who it is – and that will help you to grow up in greater love for each other.

MOTHER TERESA OF CALCUTTA

APRIL 6

It is most strange, when the great miracle
Hath for our sakes been done, when we have had
Our inwardest experience of God,
When with his presence still the room expands,
And is awed after Him, that nought is changed,
That nature's face looks unacknowledging,
And the mad world still dances heedless on.
'Tis hard at first to see it all aright;
Yet through the clouded glass
Of our own bitter tears, we learn to look
Undazzled on the kindness of God's face.

JAMES RUSSELL LOWELL

APRIL 7

Natural things are glorious, and to know them glorious. The riches of nature are our souls and bodies, with all their faculties, senses and endowments. And it had been the easiest thing in the whole world, that all felicity consisted in the enjoyment of all that world, that it was prepared for me before I was born, and that nothing was more divine and beautiful.

How strange that we forget the glory of the world around us and the glory of our own senses and faculties, says Thomas Traherne.

APRIL 8

Thanks to the human heart by which we live,
Thanks to its tenderness, its joys and fears,
To me the meanest flower that blows can give
Thoughts that do often lie too deep for tears.

WILLIAM WORDSWORTH

APRIL 9

If any point overlabour thy mind, divert and relieve it by some other subject of a more sensible or manual nature, rather than what may affect the understanding: for this were to write one thing upon another, which blots out our former impressions, or renders them illegible.

This is sound advice from William Penn, the Quaker founder of Pennsylvania. I find that physical activity like gardening or walking can sometimes relieve mental anxiety.

APRIL 10

But deep this truth impressed my mind –
Thro' all His works abroad,
The heart benevolent and kind
The most resembles God.

When I find it difficult to believe in a God that is truly loving, I think of the kind and loving people I know. This verse by Robert Burns reassures us that these are the people most like God. If ordinary folk can be kind and loving, surely God must be.

APRIL 11

A single moment of understanding can flood a whole life with meaning.

AUTHOR UNKNOWN

APRIL 12

St Francis ordered a plot to be set aside for the cultivation of flowers when the convent garden was made, in order that all who saw them might remember the Eternal Sweetness.

THOMAS OF CELANO

APRIL 13

Come to me, O ye children!
For I hear you at your play,
And the questions that perplexed me
Have vanished quite away.

For what are all our contrivings,
And the wisdom of our books,
When compared with your caresses
And the gladness of your looks?

Ye are better than all the ballads
That ever were sung or said:
For ye are living poems,
And all the rest are dead.

HENRY WADSWORTH LONGFELLOW

APRIL 14

An' many times when I do vind
Things all goo wrong, an' volk unkind,
To zee the happy veeden herds,
An' hear the zingen o' the birds,
Do soothe my sorrow more than words;
Vor I do zee that 'tis our sin
Do make one's soul so dark 'ithin,
When God would gi'e one zunsheen.

WILLIAM BARNES, THE DORSET POET

APRIL 15

I am very fond of the Quaker way of looking at things – the way beliefs are not intellectualized, can be felt not thought out. My thoughts fret me. George Fox, one of their founders, wrote this.

Be still and cool in thy own mind and spirit from thy own thoughts. Be still awhile from thy own thoughts, searching, seeking desires and imaginations, and be stayed in the principle of God in thee, that it may raise thy mind up to God, and stay it upon God, and thou will find strength from Him and find Him to be a God at hand, a present help in time of trouble and of need.

APRIL 16

The year's at the spring,
And day's at the morn;
Morning's at seven;
The hillside's dew-pearled;
The lark's on the wing;
The snail's on the thorn;
God's in His heaven –
All's right with the world!

There are some moments when suddenly everything seems right, like this Robert Browning poem. It can happen quite suddenly.

APRIL 17

Alas, the world is full of enormous lights and mysteries and man shuts them from himself with one small hand.

BAAL SHEM TOV

APRIL 18

O Human soul! so long as thou canst so
Set up a mark of everlasting light,
Above the howling senses' ebb and flow,
To cheer thee, and to right thee if thou roam –
Not with lost toil thou labourest through the night!
Thou mak'st the heaven thou hop'st indeed thy home.

MATTHEW ARNOLD

APRIL 19

Our grand business undoubtedly is not to see what lies dimly at a distance, but to do what lies clearly at hand.

THOMAS CARLYLE

APRIL 20

I must learn to accept the givenness of things around me.
I must learn to be more thankful.
I must learn to accept my own inadequacies.
I must learn to be ready to relax.
I must learn to look at the needs of others.

My brother-in-law, Father Derek Payne, a priest, gave me a piece of paper with this on it. It is the imaginative combination of things to be learned that appeals to me. A good guide for the day.

APRIL 21

Therefore, O Spirit! fearlessly bear on:
Though storms may break the primrose on its stalk,
Though frosts may blight the freshness of its bloom,
Yet spring's awakening breath will woo the earth.

PERCY BYSSHE SHELLEY

APRIL 22

He who bends to himself a joy
Doth the winged life destroy:
But he who kisses the joy as it flies
Lives in Eternity's sunrise.

What I believe William Blake is saying is that we cannot capture joy to order. Joy comes and it goes. It cannot be trapped and tied down. All we can do it is respond wholeheartedly to its arrival.

APRIL 23

The more we live by our intellect, the less we understand the meaning of life.

LEO TOLSTOI

APRIL 24

In dropping old, tired, dead thoughts and coming alive I discovered early in my own personal experience that the simple practice of outgoing love toward people is almost magically effective. Whenever I detect that my thoughts are going stale, I deliberately search for some opportunity to express love by a thoughtful and kindly act, and if I do enough of this, a new vigour, even fervour, shows in my mental state. And along with it, a revitalized feeling of aliveness and sensitivity becomes evident.

NORMAN VINCENT PEALE

APRIL 25

I love to walk the fields; they are to me
A legacy no evil can destroy;
They, like a spell, set every rapture free
That cheered me when a boy.
Play – pastime – all time's blotting
  pen concealed,
Comes like a newborn joy
To greet me in the field.

JOHN CLARE

APRIL 26

Nay I see that God is in all creatures, man and beast, fish and fowl, and every green thing from the highest cedar to the ivy on the wall; and that God is the life and being of them all. So he may well be said to be everywhere, as he is; and so I cannot exclude him from man or beast, or any other creature, and there is no difference betwixt man and beast but as man carries a more lively image of the divine being.

This idea, expressed by a seventeenth-century writer Jacob Bauthumley, that God is not far away in some heaven apart from us but is in us, near us, all around us, makes me feel less lonely.

APRIL 27

Deeds from love, and words, that flow
Foster like kind April showers;
In the warm sun all things grow,
Wholesome fruits and pleasant flowers:
All so thrive his gentle rays
Whereon human love displays.

Thomas Campion says love works on human beings like sun and April showers work on plants – making them grow and flower.

APRIL 28

When all is done and said,
In the end thus shall you find,
He most of all doth bathe in bliss
That hath a quiet mind:
And, clear from worldly cares,
Can deem to be content
The sweetest time in all his life
In thinking to be spent.

LORD VAUX

APRIL 29

A single gentle rain makes the grass many shades greener. So our prospects brighten on the influx of better thoughts. We should be blessed if we lived in the present always, and took advantage of every accident that befell us, like the grass which confesses the influence of the slightest dew that falls on it; and did not spend our time in atoning for the neglect of past opportunities, which we call doing our duty. We loiter in winter while it is already spring.

HENRY DAVID THOREAU

APRIL 30

O to be up and doing, O
Unfearing and unshamed to go
In all the uproar and the press
About my human business!
My undissuaded heart I hear
Whisper courage in my ear.

ROBERT LOUIS STEVENSON

MAY

May, thou month of rosy beauty,
May, when pleasure is a duty.
Month of bees, and month of flowers,
Month of blossom-laden bowers;
Month of little hands with daisies,
Lovers' love and poets' praises;
O thou merry month complete,
May, thy very name is sweet!
May's the blooming hawthorn bough;
May's the month that's laughing now.

MAY 1

It is a dull heart indeed that cannot find either comfort or joy in the sheer beauty of nature this month. For as Leigh Hunt's little poem suggests, it is almost a duty to enjoy the blossom and bees and stirrings of summer around us in both city and country.

MAY 2

Think earnestly of the witness which joy on the one hand, and its antithesis, boredom, on the other, bear to the duty and happiness of creative work, that is to say real work, on however small a scale. Boredom is a certain sign that we are allowing our best faculties to rust in idleness. When people are bored, they generally look about for a new pleasure, or take a holiday. What they want is some hard piece of work.

Boredom is a sign that something is wrong with the human life, says William Inge. Wear out, don't rust out, my father used to say.

MAY 3 *The American poet, James Russell Lowell, wrote a moving poem to the common dandelion. What beauty there is in a weed, if we see it.*

Dear common flower, that grow'st beside the way,
Fringing the dusty road with harmless gold,
First pledge of blithesome May,
Which children pluck, and full of pride, uphold.
How like a prodigal doth nature seem,
When thou, for all thy gold so common art!
Thou teachest me to deem
More sacredly of every human heart,
Since each reflects in joy its scanty gleam
Of heaven.

MAY 4 What is love?
It is the sweetness
of life; it is the sweet,
tender, melting nature of God,
flowing up through his seed of
life into the creature, and of all things making the creature most like unto himself, both in nature and operation. It excludes all evil out of the heart, it perfects all good in the heart. A touch of love doth this in measure; perfect love doth this in fulness.

ISAAC PENINGTON

MAY 5

True wisdom consists in knowing one's duty exactly. True piety in acting what one knows. To aim at more than this, is to run into endless mistakes.

BISHOP THOMAS WILSON

MAY 6

O solitude, the soul's best friend.
How calm and quiet a delight
        It is alone
To read, and meditate, and write,
By none offended nor offending none;
To walk, ride, sit, or sleep at one's own ease,
And pleasing a man's self, none other to displease.

During a hectic life we need times to be alone with ourselves. Charles Cotton's poem describes how solitude can renew us.

MAY 7

I do not know wherein I could be better than the worm. For see: he does the will of his Maker and destroys nothing.

RABBI MENDEL

MAY 8

I wish but what I have at will;
I wander not to seek for more;
I like the plain, I climb no hill;
In greatest storms I sit on shore,
And laugh at them that toil in vain
To get what must be lost again.

SIR EDWARD DYER

MAY 9

All my hurts
My garden spade can heal. A woodland walk,
A quest of river grapes, a mocking thrush,
A wild rose, a rock-loving columbine,
Salve my worst wounds.

RALPH WALDO EMERSON

MAY 10 All that have meant good work with their whole hearts have done good work. Every heart that has beat strong and cheerfully has left a hopeful impulse behind it in the world, and bettered the tradition of mankind.

ROBERT LOUIS STEVENSON

MAY 11 *There's a lovely poem by Robert Bridges about the burden of having. Real sorrow is less painful than our imaginary ones.*

Since pleasure with the having disappeareth,
He who hath least in hand hath most at heart
While he keep hope: as he who alway feareth
A grief that never comes hath yet the smart;
And heavier far is our self-wrought distress,
For when God sendeth sorrow, it doth bless.

MAY 12 Let us be more loving, more indulgent towards each other – we are all so much in need of mutual love and help, and all our difficulties and sorrows are so insignificant in the face of eternity.

FATHER ALEXANDER ELCHANINOV

MAY 13

Tumult and turmoil, trouble and toil,
Yet peace withal in a painful heart;
Never a grudge and never a broil,
And ever the better part.

O my King and my heart's own choice,
Stretch Thy hand to Thy fluttering dove;
Teach me, call to me with Thy voicc,
Wrap me up in Thy love.

Christina Rossetti's poem strives for a loving acceptance in trouble and I particularly love its comforting last line.

MAY 14

No man can tell, but he that loves his children, how many delicious accents make a man's heart dance in the pretty conversation of those dear pledges; their childishness, their stammerings, their little angers, their innocence, their imperfections, their necessities are so many little emanations of joy and comfort to him that delights in their persons and society.

JEREMY TAYLOR

MAY 15

You say that this world to you seems drained of all its sweets! O Robert, I don't know what you call sweet. Honey and the honeycomb, roses and violets, are yet in the earth. The sun and moon yet reign in heaven and the lesser lights keep up their pretty twinkling. Meats and drinks, sweet sights and sweet smells, a country walk, spring and autumn, follies and repentance, quarrels and reconcilements, have all a sweetness by turn. Good humour and good nature, friends at home that love you, you possess all these things, and more innumerable, and these are all sweet things. You may extract honey from everything; do not go gathering after gall. The bees are wiser in their generation than the race of complainers. I assure you I find this world a very pretty place.

CHARLES LAMB

MAY 16

Where with intention I have erred,
No other plea I have,
But Thou art good; and goodness still
Delighteth to forgive.

ROBERT BURNS

I pray for faith, I long to trust;
I listen with my heart, and hear
A Voice without a sound: 'Be just,
Be true, be merciful, revere
The Word within thee: God is near.'

MAY 17

JOHN GREENLEAF WHITTIER

If we have thus desecrated ourselves – as who has not? – the remedy will be by wariness and devotion to reconsecrate ourselves. Read not *The Times*. Read the Eternities. Conventionalities are at length as bad as impurities. Knowledge does not come to us by details, but in flashes of light from heaven. Yes, every thought that passes through the mind helps to deepen the ruts which evince how much it has been used.

MAY 18

HENRY DAVID THOREAU

Flower in the crannied wall,
I pluck you out of the crannies,
I hold you here, root and all, in my hand,
Little flower – but if I could understand
What you are, root and all, and all in all,
I should know what God and man is.

MAY 19

ALFRED, LORD TENNYSON

Without the desert, there is no oasis.

MAY 20

ABRAHAM BARZALI

MAY 21 *The poet and mystic William Blake wrote a whole series of proverbs to help us see life in a new way. Here are some of them.*

Damn braces, bless relaxes.
No bird soars too high, if he soars with his own wings.
Exuberance is beauty.
He whose face gives no light shall never become a star.

MAY 22

My own heart let me more have pity on; let
Me live to my sad self hereafter kind.

GERARD MANLEY HOPKINS

MAY 23 While trying to make provision for yourselves and your families, be not anxious overmuch, but in quietness of spirit seek first the Kingdom of God. Be ready, in response to the divine call, to save or to spend, to give or to bequeath; to one the summons is to bring fresh energy and vision into his work; to another to limit his engagements or even to retire from business, that he may be free for new service.

THE QUAKER GENERAL ADVICES

MAY 24

Oh! let me then at length be taught
What I am still so slow to learn,
That God is love, and changes not,
Nor knows the shadow of a turn.

This is a verse from the hymns written by William Cowper when he was trying to recover from inner despair and self-hatred.

Conquer by accepting. Pain, like other elemental forces in nature, can be turned to use but only if the laws of its operation are first understood and conformed to. Those who meet it clear-eyed and with a positive and active acceptance make a strange discovery. They find that they achieve an enrichment and a growth of personality which makes them centres of influence and light. They become socially creative. MAY 25

BURNET HILLMAN STREETER

William Wordsworth wrote several poems to the humble daisy. He felt it had a kind of a lesson for mankind. The daisy flourishes because it grows low and is thus sheltered from bad weather. MAY 26

Bright flower! whose home is everywhere,
Bold in maternal Nature's care,
And all the long year through the heir
   Of joy and sorrow;
Methinks that there abides in thee
Some concord with humanity,
Given to no other flower I see
   The forest thorough!

MAY 27

The nature writer Richard Jefferies believed that the pigeons and doves found in city and country have a lesson for restless man.

They have not laboured in mental searching as we have; they have not wasted their time looking among empty straw for the grain that is not there. They have been in the sunlight. Since the days of ancient Greece the doves have remained in the sunshine; we who have laboured have found nothing. In the sunshine, by the shady verge of the woods, by the sweet waters where the wild dove sips, there alone will thought be found.

MAY 28

Nor land nor yet living belongs unto me,
Yet I can go out in the meadows and see
The healthy green grass – and behold the shower fall,
As the wealth of that being that blesses us all.
And he that feels this, who can say he is poor?
For fortune's the birthright of joy – nothing more.
And he that feels thus takes the wealth from the soil,
For the miser owns nought but the trouble and toil.

As John Clare says, we need not own things to enjoy them.

Consider how, even in the meanest sorts of labour, the whole soul of a man is composed into a kind of real harmony, the instant he sets himself to work! Doubt, desire, sorrow, remorse, indignation, despair itself, all these like helldogs lie beleaguering the soul of the poor dayworker, as of every man: but he bends himself with free valour against his task, and all these are stilled, all these shrink murmuring far off into their caves. MAY 29

THOMAS CARLYLE

Father, give to us and to all your people, MAY 30
In times of anxiety, serenity;
In times of hardship, courage;
In times of uncertainty, patience;
And at all times a quiet trust in your wisdom and love.

I do not know who wrote this Church of England prayer. I heard it one evensong. It seems to me to sum up what I need for happiness.

Among the mind's powers is one that comes of itself to many children and artists. It need not be lost, to the end of his days, by anyone who has ever had it. This is the power of taking delight in a thing, or rather in anything, not as a means to some other end, but just because it is what it is. A child in the full health of his mind will put his hand flat on the summer turf, feel it, and give a little shiver of private glee at the elastic firmness of the globe. MAY 31

CHARLES EDWARD MONTAGUE

JUNE

JUNE 1

The sheer beauty of this month of June helps heal any unhappiness that I feel. What I like about this poem by James Russell Lowell is that he remembers not just how beautiful the sights of June are, but also how beautiful are the sounds.

Oh! what is so rare as a day in June?
Then, if ever, come perfect days;
Then Heaven tries the earth if it be in tune,
And over it softly her warm ear lays:
Whether we look, or whether we listen,
We hear life murmur, or see it glisten.
Now the heart is so full that a drop overfills it,
We are happy now because God wills it.
No matter how barren the past may have been,
'Tis enough for us now that the leaves are green.

JUNE 2

Dive deep into thy bosom; learn the depth, extent, bias, and full fort of thy mind; contract full intimacy with the stranger within thee; excite and cherish every spark of intellectual light, however smothered under former negligence, or scattered through the full, dark mass of common thoughts; I say 'Reverence thyself.'

So often in my struggle to live at ease with myself I have been frightened to look within and know my true self. I have thought myself such a worthless person instead of reverencing myself, faults and virtues, as Edward Young the writer and poet suggests.

JUNE 3 *Frederick William Harvey was an English poet whose poems, written before the last World War, are now forgotten, except for this one. This was his masterpiece – touching, true and funny.*

From troubles of the world
  I turn to ducks,
Beautiful comic things
Sleeping or curled
Their heads beneath white wings
By water cool,
Or finding curious things
To eat in various mucks
Beneath the pool,
Tails uppermost, or waddling
Sailor-like on the shores
Of ponds, or paddling
– Left! right – with fanlike feet.

JUNE 4 Real difficulties can be overcome; it is only the imaginary ones that are unconquerable.

THEODORE N. VAIL

JUNE 5

This passage comes from the will of Sydney Cockerell. I know nothing about him except these lovely words, which were passed on to me by a dear friend Valerie Finnis, who fulfils their spirit.

I have been blessed throughout my long life with a number of the dearest kindest friends, both men and women, that man ever had. Gratefully conscious of all they have meant to me, I declare friendship to be precious beyond all words. But it is like a plant that withers if it be not heedfully tended. It must be fostered by means of visits, of letters, of little services and attentions, and by constant thought, sympathy and kindness. I implore my children and my grandchildren to remember this.

JUNE 6

It is right it should be so,
Man was made for joy and woe;
And when this we rightly know
Through the world we safely go.

William Blake's simple little verse has a profound message. Pain accepted is pain transfigured. Without pain we cannot know joy.

JUNE 7

Why should we be in such desperate haste to succeed, and in such desperate enterprises? If a man cannot keep pace with his companions, perhaps it is because he hears a different drummer. Let him step to the music which he hears, however measured or far away. We will not be shipwrecked on a vain reality.

HENRY DAVID THOREAU

JUNE 8 All joys hail from paradise, and jests too, provided they are uttered in true joy.

RABBI PINHAS

JUNE 9

All creatures and all objects, in degree,
Are friends and patrons of humanity.
There are to whom the garden, grove and field
Perpetual lessons of forbearance yield;
Who would not lightly violate the grace
The lowliest flower possesses in its place,
Nor shorten the sweet life, too fugitive,
Which nothing less than Infinite Power could give.

William Wordsworth felt nature was sacred. This feeling was so strong he hesitated to pick a flower. We need to hear his message.

JUNE 10 I can tell you for an eternal truth that troubled souls are always safe. Trouble in itself is always a claim on love, and God is love. It is the prisoners, and the blind and the leper, and the possessed, and the hungry and the tempest-tossed, who are His special care. Therefore if you are lost and sick and bound, you are just in the place where He can meet you.

ANDREW JUKES

JUNE 11

God imparteth by the way
Strength sufficient for the day.

J. E. SAXBY

Happiness and beauty are by-products. Folly is the direct pursuit of happiness and beauty. JUNE 12

BERNARD SHAW

Summer is prodigal of joy. The grass JUNE 13
Swarms with delighted insects as I pass,
And crowds of grasshoppers at every stride
Jump out all ways with happiness their guide;
And from my brushing feet moths flirt away
In safer places to pursue their play.
In crowds they start. I marvel, well I may,
To see such worlds of insects in the way,
And more to see each thing, however small,
Sharing joy's bounty that belongs to all.
And here I gather, by the world forgot,
Harvests of comfort from their happy mood,
Feeling God's blessing dwells in every spot
And nothing lives but owes him gratitude.

John Clare, the son of a farm labourer, is one of the greatest English poets, yet he died almost forgotten in an insane asylum.

JUNE 14

It is not only prayer that gives God glory but work. Smiting on an anvil, sawing a beam, whitewashing a wall, driving horses, sweeping, scouring, everything gives God some glory if being in his grace you do it as your duty. To lift up the hands in prayer gives God glory, but a man with a dungfork in his hand, a woman with a sloppail, give him glory too. He is so great that all things give him glory if you mean they should.

This passage comes from a sermon by Gerard Manley Hopkins. I often work in haste. Remembering God's glory can slow me down.

JUNE 15

The roses fauld their silken leaves,
The foxglove shuts its bell;
The honeysuckle and the birk
Spread fragrance through the dell.
Let others crowd the giddy court
Of mirth and revelry,
The simple joys that Nature yields
Are dearer far to me.

ROBERT TANNAHILL

JUNE 16

Were all the year one constant sunshine, we
   Should have no flowers,
All would be drought and leanness; not a tree
   Would make us bowers;
Beauty consists in colours; and that's best
Which is not fixed, but flies and flowers.

I fear change. I want good times to last for ever. Yet unalloyed pleasure is bad for human beings, like too much sun for flowers as the seventeenth-century poet Henry Vaughan points out.

JUNE 17

By desiring what is perfectly good, even when we don't quite know what it is and cannot do what we would, we are part of the divine power against evil – widening the skirts of light and making the struggle with darkness narrower.

GEORGE ELIOT

JUNE 18

Nature ne'er deserts the wise and pure;
No plot so narrow, be but nature there,
No waste so vacant, but may well employ
Each faculty of sense and keep the heart
Awake to love and beauty.

SAMUEL TAYLOR COLERIDGE

JUNE 19

Even a slug is a star if it dares to be its horned and slimy self.

JOHN HARGRAVE

JUNE 20 The past exists only in memory, consequences, effects. It has power over me only as I give it my power. I can let go, release it, move freely. I am not my past.

AUTHOR UNKNOWN

JUNE 21 *In early summer trees, plants and fields turn deep true green. These lines by the poet Gerard Benson suggest the joy of a colour.*

And still the green, folding in from the wooded hillsides,
The birch leaves and the oak leaves green;
The green grass, starred with tiny white flowers
And small buttercups. Green.
And the dense light from the conifers,
Green. And the quiet slopping lake water muddy green.

JUNE 22 It is the heart that is not yet sure of its God that is afraid to laugh in His presence.

GEORGE MACDONALD

JUNE 23 *Sometimes I need comforting by a hug. I bought a card with this anonymous verse. It's awful doggerel but I like its message.*

It's wondrous what a hug can do,
A hug can cheer you when you're blue.
A hug can soothe a small child's pain
And bring a rainbow after rain.
A hug delights and warms,
It must be why God gave us arms.

JUNE 24

Do not trouble yourself about your troubles, do not be uneasy about your uneasiness; do not be discouraged because you are discouraged, but return immediately to God.

When I am troubled, I add to that trouble by blaming myself for it. I need to bear in mind this advice from Jean Paul Caussade.

JUNE 25

We thank Thee, Lord of Heaven,
For all that Thou hast given
To help and to delight us.
For friends who gladly greet us,
For flowers of field and garden,
For bees with sweetness laden,
For swift and gallant horses,
For dogs with friendly faces,
For homely dwelling places,
For song and kindly voices,
For good and sleep and ease,
We thank Thee, Lord, for these.

AUTHOR UNKNOWN

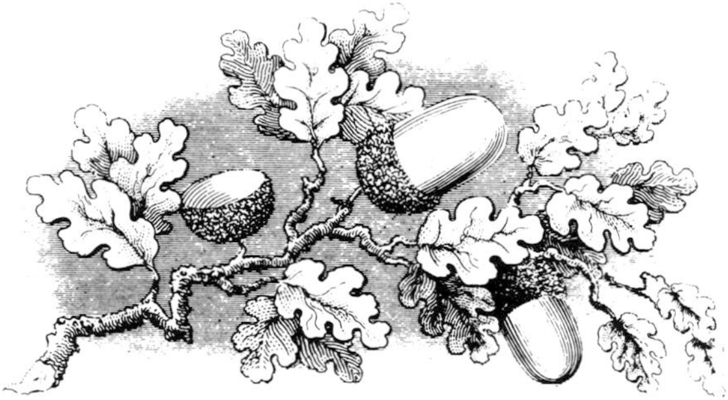

JUNE 26 Let not the eyes grow dim, look not back but forward; the soul must uphold itself like the sun. Let us labour to make the heart grow larger as we become older, as the spreading oak gives more shelter. That we could but take to the soul some of the greatness and the beauty of the summer!

RICHARD JEFFERIES

JUNE 27 For the whole world before thee is as a little grain of the
balance, yea, as a drop of the morning dew that falleth
down upon the earth.
For thou lovest all the things that are, and abhorrest nothing
which thou has made: for never wouldst thou have made
anything, if thou hadst hated it.
And how could any thing have endured, if it had not been
thy will? Or been preserved if not called by thee?
But thou sparest all: for they are thine, O Lord, thou
lover of souls.

This moving passage from the Wisdom of Solomon in the Apocrypha comforts me by reminding me that a loving God does not make rubbish. None of us were created to be thrown away.

JUNE 28

If a thousand plans fail, be not disheartened. As long as your purposes are right, *you* have not failed.

THOMAS DAVIDSON

JUNE 29

All we have willed or hoped or dreamed of good shall
  exist;
Not in semblance, but itself; no beauty, nor good, nor
  power,
Whose voice has gone forth, but each survives for the
  melodist
When eternity affirms the conception of an hour.
The high that proved too high, the heroic for earth too
  hard,
The passion that left the ground to lose itself in the
  sky,
Are music sent up to God by the lover and the bard;
Enough that He heard it once: we shall hear it by and
  by.

ROBERT BROWNING

JUNE 30

Let us not therefore go hurrying about and collecting honey, bee-like, buzzing here and there impatiently from a knowledge of what is to be arrived at. But let us open out leaves like a flower, and be passive and receptive: budding patiently under the eye of Apollo and taking hints from every noble insect that favours us with a visit.

JOHN KEATS

JULY

JULY 1

Thou perceivest the flowers put forth their precious
odours!
And none can tell how from so small a centre comes
such sweets
Forgetting that within that centre eternity expands
Its ever during doors ...
First e'er the morning breaks, joy opens in the flowery
bosoms,
Joy even to tears, which the sun rising dries; first the
wild thyme
And meadowsweet, downy and soft waving among
the reeds,
Light springing on the air lead the sweet dance: they
wake
The honeysuckle sleeping on the oak: the flaunting
beauty revels along upon the wind.

Eternity expands from the centre of a flower, says William Blake. Let me remember this when I walk in gardens, parks or fields.

JULY 2

Whatever falls upon us from that Almighty hand, it is a diamond. It is the matter of some new blessing, if we abuse it not. Be pleased to remember that there are bright stars under the most palpable clouds, and light is never so beautiful as in the presence of darkness.

HENRY VAUGHAN

JULY 3 All real and wholesome enjoyments possible to man have been just as possible to him, since first he was made of the earth, as they are now: and they are possible to him chiefly in peace. To watch the corn grow, and the blossoms set; to draw hard breath over ploughshare or spade; to read, to think, to love, to hope, to pray – these are the things that make men happy.

JOHN RUSKIN

JULY 4

I know not how it is with you
I love the first and last,
The whole field of the present view,
The whole flow of the past.

One tittle of the things that are,
Nor you should change nor I –
One pebble in our path – one star
In all our heaven of sky.

I love this poem by Robert Louis Stevenson because just accepting and loving things as they are is a struggle. At times I battle against feelings of unease, as if I lived against the grain of life.

JULY 5

This passage by Arthur Benson gave me an new idea for my daily meditation. I imagine cows lying chewing the cud, and feel calmed.

Cows bring a deep tranquillity into the spirit; their glossy skins, their fragrant breath, their contented ease, their mild gaze, their Epicurean rumination tend to restore the balance of the mind.

JULY 6

O Joy, that seekest me through pain,
I cannot close my heart to Thee;
I trace the rainbow through the rain,
And feel the promise is not vain
That morn shall tearless be.

GEORGE MATHESON

JULY 7

Do not be in a hurry to fill up an empty space with words and embellishments, before it has been filled with a deep interior peace.

FATHER ALEXANDER ELCHANINOV

JULY 8

No, when the fight begins within himself,
A man's worth something. God stoops o'er his head,
Satan looks up between his feet – both tug –
He's left, himself, in the middle; the soul wakes
And grows. Prolong that battle through his life!
Never leave growing till the life to come!

Robert Browning's lines remind me that sometimes when I am in inner turmoil, I need to be. Conflict can be a sign of inner growth.

JULY 9 Love is a fruit in season at all times, and within the reach of every hand. Anyone may gather it and no limit is set. Everyone can reach this love through meditation, spirit of prayer, and sacrifice, by an intense inner life.

MOTHER TERESA OF CALCUTTA

JULY 10 *When I must have dealings with difficult people or at times of family disagreements, I try to recall this verse by Hilaire Belloc.*

Of courtesy, it is much less
Than courage of heart or holiness,
Yet in my walks it seems to me
That the grace of God is in courtesy.

JULY 11 I think that we may safely trust a good deal more than we do. The incessant anxiety and strain of some is a well-nigh incurable form of disease. We are made to exaggerate the importance of what work we do; and yet how much is not done by us! How vigilant we are! determined not to live by faith if we can avoid it.

HENRY DAVID THOREAU

JULY 12 I cannot hold Thee fast, though Thou art mine:
Hold Thou me fast,
So earth shall know at last and heaven at last
That I am Thine.

CHRISTINA ROSSETTI

JULY 13

O God, early in the morning I cry to you.
Help me to pray
And to concentrate my thoughts on you ...
In me there is darkness,
But with you there is light;
I am lonely, but you do not leave me;
I am feeble in heart, but with you there is help;
I am restless, but with you there is peace.
In me there is bitterness, but with you there is patience;
I do not understand your ways
But you know the way for me.

This prayer was made by the German Protestant minister Dietrich Bonhoeffer, as he awaited execution in a Nazi prison.

JULY 14

From the child you can learn three things. He is merry for no particular reason; never for a moment is he idle; when he needs something, he demands it vigorously.

THE MAGGID OF MEZRITCH

JULY 15 The dog is a saint. He is straightforward and honest by nature. He knows by instinct when he is not wanted; lies quite still for hours when his king is hard at work. But when his king is sad and worried he knows that his time has come, and he creeps up and lays his head on his lap. 'Don't worry. Never mind if they all abandon you. Let us go for a walk and forget all about it!'

AXEL MUNTHE

JULY 16

Now, almost hid in trees, a little gate
Cheats us into the darkness of the wood.
We almost think the day is wearing late
So dreamy is the light that dwells around.
And so refreshing is its sombre mood,
We feel at once shut out from sun and sky,
All the deliciousness of solitude,
While sauntering noiseless o'er the leafy ground
The air we breathe seems loosing every trace
Of earth and all its trouble.

John Clare is right. A walk in the wood can banish our anxieties.

JULY 17

It's sometimes difficult to walk along the less trodden way. People, even loved ones, want you to conform. Ralph Waldo Emerson has some words for those of us who need comforting in our path.

We pass for what we are. Be it how it will, do right now. Always scorn appearances, and you always may. The force of character is cumulative. All the foregone days of virtue work their health into this.

JULY 18

Go with events,
Rather than strive against them;
Work on your virtues,
Rather than your faults.

AUTHOR UNKNOWN

JULY 19

Try not to feel good when thou art not good, but cry to Him who is good. He has an especial tenderness of love toward thee for that thou art in the dark and hast no light, and His heart is glad when thou dost say, 'I will go to my Father.' Fold the arms of thy faith, and wait in the quietness until light goes up in thy darkness.

GEORGE MACDONALD

JULY 20

The rose that with your earthly eyes you see,
Has flowered in God from all eternity.

I find it both comforting and inspiring to try to see signs of the divine in the ordinary. I can see God in a rose from my garden or wild in the hedge, according to this couplet by Angelus Silesius.

JULY 21

Think deeply;
Speak gently;
Love much;
Laugh often;
Work hard;
Give freely;
Pay promptly:
Be kind.

ANONYMOUS

JULY 22 Neither go back in fear and misgiving to the past, nor in anxiety and forecasting to the future; but lie quiet under His hand, having no will but His.

CARDINAL HENRY MANNING

JULY 23

Kind words toward those you daily meet,
Kind words and actions right,
Will make this life of ours most sweet,
Turn darkness into light.

ISAAC WATTS

JULY 24 If we had never before looked upon the earth, but suddenly came to it man or woman grown, set down in the midst of a summer mead, would it not seem to us a radiant vision? The mind would be filled with its glory, unable to grasp it.

RICHARD JEFFERIES

JULY 25

O heart, hold thee secure
In this blind hour of stress,
Live on, love on, endure,
Uncowed, though comfortless.

Life's still the wondrous thing
It seemed in bygone peace,
Though woe now jar the string
And all its music cease.

WALTER DE LA MARE

JULY 26

Nature sings her exquisite song to the artist, alone. To him her secrets are unfolded. He looks at her flower not with the enlarging lens, that he may gather facts for the botanist, but with the light of one who sees in her choice selection of brilliant tones and delicate tints, suggestions of future harmonies. In the long curve of the narrow leaf, corrected by the straight tall stem, he learns how grace is wedded to dignity, how strength enhances sweetness.

The artist James Whistler reminds us to notice beauty around us.

JULY 27 *We cannot passively leave all to God. We must do our part. The prophet Mohammed once overheard one of his followers say that he would untie his camel and commit it to God. He said to the man:*

Friend, tie your camel and
commit it to God.

JULY 28

It's no in titles nor in rank;
It's no in wealth like Lon'on bank,
To purchase peace and rest;
It's no in making muckle, *mair*:
It's no in books, it's no in lear,
To make us truly blest.
If happiness hae not her seat
And centre in the breast,
We may be wise, or rich, or great,
But never can be blest;
Nae treasures, nor pleasures,
Could make us happy lang;
The heart ay's the part ay,
That makes us right or wrang.

ROBERT BURNS

JULY 29

First ask yourself, is this my problem? If it isn't leave it alone. If it is my problem, can I tackle it now? Do so. If your problem could be settled by an expert in some field, go quickly to him and take his advice.

I've found this advice from Dr Austen Riggs useful when I am worrying. Often it is not my problem, and I need to let go of it.

JULY 30

Ah, quiet, all things feel thy balm!
Those blue hills too, this river's flow,
Were restless once, but long ago.
Tamed is their turbulent youthful glow;
Their joy is in their calm.

There are few poems in praise of quietness, perhaps because it is difficult to describe calm. Matthew Arnold succeeds, I think.

JULY 31

God has created me to do Him some definite service; He has committed some work to me which He has not committed to another. I have my mission – I may never know it in this life, but I shall be told it in the next. I am a link in a chain, a bond of connection between persons. He has not created me for naught. I shall do good, I shall do His work. Therefore I will trust Him. Whatever, wherever I am, I can never be thrown away. If I am in sickness, my sickness may serve Him; in perplexity, my perplexity may serve Him; if I am in sorrow, my sorrow may serve Him. He does nothing in vain. He knows what He is about.

CARDINAL JOHN NEWMAN

AUGUST

AUGUST 1

Love bade me welcome; yet my soul drew back,
   Guilty of dust and sin.
But quick-eyed Love, observing me grow slack
   From my first entrance in,
Drew nearer to me, sweetly questioning
   If I lacked anything.

'A guest,' I answered, 'worthy to be here;'
   Love said, 'You shall be he.'
'I, the unkind, ungrateful? Ah, my dear,
   I cannot look on Thee.'
Love took my hand, and smiling did reply.
   'Who made the eyes but I?'

'Truth, Lord; but I have marred them; let my shame
   Go where it doth deserve.'
'And know you not,' says Love, 'Who bore the blame?'
   'My dear, then I will serve.'
'You must sit down,' says Love, 'And taste My meat.'
   So I did sit and eat.

Sometimes it is hard to accept love. George Herbert's poem tells me that I must accept love and allow it to work its healing on me.

AUGUST 2

Worry and gloom are the roots of all the powers of evil.

RABBI JACOB JOSEPH

AUGUST

AUGUST 3

Man only plays when, in the full meaning of the word, he is a man, and he is only completely a man when he plays.

FRIEDRICH SCHILLER

AUGUST 4

Field thoughts to me are happiness and joy,
Where I can lie upon the pleasant grass,
Or track some little path and so employ
My mind in trifles, pausing as I pass
The little wild flower clumps by, nothing nursed
But dews and sunshine and impartial rain;
And welcomely to quench my summer thirst
I bend me by the flaggy dyke to gain
Dewberries so delicious to the taste;
And then I wind the flag-fringed meadow lake
And mark the pike plunge with unusual haste
Through waterweeds and many a circle make,
While bursts of happiness from heaven fall; –
There all have hopes: here fields are free for all.

JOHN CLARE

Work is not always required of a man. There is such a thing as sacred idleness, the cultivation of which is now fearfully neglected. AUGUST 5

GEORGE MACDONALD

Oh, the little birds sang east, and the little birds sang
west, AUGUST 6
And I smiled to think God's greatness flowed around our
incompleteness –
Round our restlessness, His rest.

ROBERT BROWNING

Be patterns, be examples in all countries, places, islands, nations, wherever you come: that your carriage and life may preach among all sorts of people, and to them; then you will come to walk cheerfully over the world, answering that of God in every one. AUGUST 7

Quaker George Fox, sent this message from prison. He talks of walking over, not in, the world, and of finding God in each person.

Joy, Lady, is the spirit and the power, AUGUST 8
Which wedding nature gives to us in dower,
A new earth and new heaven,
Undreamt of by the sensual and the proud –
Joy is the sweet voice, joy the luminous cloud –
We in ourselves rejoice.

SAMUEL TAYLOR COLERIDGE

AUGUST 9

Concern should drive us into action and not into depression.

KAREN HORNEY

AUGUST 10

Thou seest the gorgeous clothed flies that dance and
  sport in summer
Upon the sunny brooks and meadows: every one the
  dance
Knows in its intricate mazes of delight artful to weave:
Each one to sound his instruments of music in the
  dance,
To touch each other and recede, to cross and change and
  return ...
These the visions of eternity.

Even the midges are part of heaven around us, to William Blake.

AUGUST 11

It is the child's spirit, which we are most happy when we most recover; remaining wiser than children in our gratitude that we can still be pleased with a fair colour or a dancing light.

JOHN RUSKIN

AUGUST 12

You have to live on this twenty-four hours of daily time. Out of it you have to spin health, pleasure, money, content, respect and the evolution of your immortal soul. Its right use, its most effective use, is a matter of the highest urgency and of the most thrilling actuality. All depends on that. We shall never have any more time.

Arnold Bennett says time should not be wasted. How sad it would be to feel there was too much time. I feel never feel there is enough.

AUGUST 13

But He will never meake our sheare
O' sorrow mwore than we can bear,
But meake us zee, if 'tis His will,
That He can bring us good vrom ill.

WILLIAM BARNES, THE DORSET POET

AUGUST 14

I have seen
A curious child, who dwelt upon a tract
Of inland ground, applying to his ear
The convolutions of a smooth-lipped shell:
To which, in silence hushed, his very soul
Listened intensely; and his countenance soon
Brightened with joy, for from within were heard
Murmurings, whereby the monitor expressed
Mysterious union with its native sea.
Even such a shell the universe itself
Is to the ear of faith.

WILLIAM WORDSWORTH

AUGUST 15

The poetry of the earth is never dead:
When all the birds are faint with the hot sun,
That is the grasshopper's – he takes the lead
In summer luxury, – he has never done
With his delights; for when tired out with fun
He rests at ease beneath some pleasant weed.

In the high summer it is marvellous just to stop and listen to the noises around you. In the countryside you can hear, just like the poet John Keats, the grasshoppers. You will also hear the buzz of a thousand small insects – bees, wasps, flies. Even in a park you can sometimes hear them through the traffic noise. This is the earth's poetry, heard only by those who listen for its harmonies.

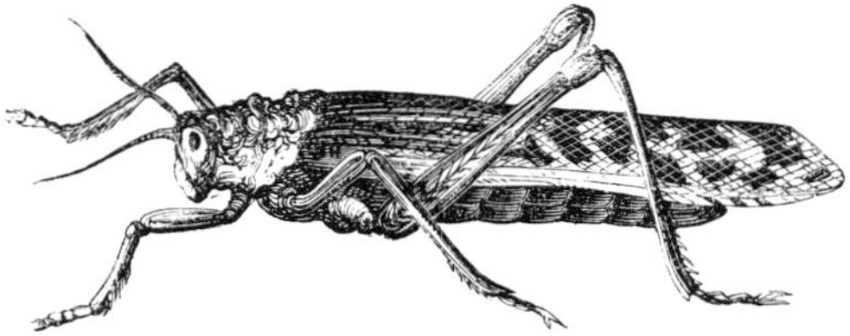

AUGUST 16

I was in the Royal Automobile Club, of all places, on an afternoon that summer, and my eye happened to fall on a door. It was quite an ordinary door, in so far as any single thing in the universe is ordinary, with small panels and big panels and a knob; but I tell you that this door, and the look and the sound and the life of it, filled me with joy inexpressible.

VICTOR GOLLANCZ

AUGUST 17

He hath but a weak eye, that sees not the sparkling beams of eternity, darting out their refulgent beauty in and through variety.

JOSEPH SALMON

AUGUST 18

Speak nought, move not, but listen, the sky is full of
gold.
No ripple on the river, no stir in field or fold,
All gleams but nought doth glisten, but the far-off
unseen sea.

Forget days past, heart broken, put all memory by!
No grief on the green hillside, no pity in the sky,
Joy that may not be spoken fills mead and flower and
tree.

WILLIAM MORRIS

AUGUST 19

Fear builds walls; love builds bridges.

AUTHOR UNKNOWN

AUGUST 20

I fear no more. The clouded face
Of nature smiles; through all her things
Of time and space and sense I trace
The moving of the Spirit's wings,
And hear the song of hope she sings.

JOHN GREENLEAF WHITTIER

AUGUST 21

And because all those scattered rays of beauty and loveliness which we behold spread up and down over all the world, are only the emanations of that inexhausted light which is above; therefore should we love them all in that, and climb up always, by those sunbeams, unto the eternal Father of Lights.

John Smith

AUGUST 22

When all within is peace,
 How nature seems to smile!
Delights that never cease,
 The live-long day beguile.

William Cowper

AUGUST 23

These words from Sir Humphrey Davy, the Victorian scientist, were chosen by Britain's Margaret Thatcher for an anthology.

Life is not made up of great sacrifices and duties but of little things: in which smiles and kindness given habitually are what win and preserve the heart and secure comfort.

AUGUST 24

To me every hour of the light and dark is a miracle ...
To me the sea is a continual miracle,
The fishes that swim – the rocks – the motion of the
 waves – the ships with men in them
What stranger miracles are there?

Walt Whitman

AUGUST 25

I find it difficult to trust God because I find it hard to believe in a truly loving God. This hymn by Frederick Faber says what I need.

There's a wideness in God's mercy,
  Like the wideness of the sea;
There's a kindness in his justice,
  Which is more than liberty.
But we make His love too narrow
  By false limits of our own;
And we magnify his strictness
  With a zeal He will not own.

AUGUST 26

The corn was orient and immortal wheat, which never should be reaped nor was ever sown. I thought it had stood from everlasting to everlasting. The gates were at first the end of the world; the green trees when I saw them first through one of the gates transported and ravished me; their sweetness and unusual beauty made my heart to leap, and almost mad with ecstasy, they were such strange and wonderful things.

Thomas Traherne is describing how he saw the world, when he was a child – a vision that we should try to recapture as adults.

AUGUST 27

See what a lovely shell,
Small and pure as a pearl,
Lying close to my foot,
Frail, but a work divine,
Made so fairily well
With delicate spire and whorl,
How exquisitely minute,
A miracle of design.

What is it? a learned man
Could give it a clumsy name.
Let him name it who can,
The beauty would be the same.

ALFRED, LORD TENNYSON

AUGUST 28

Man must be lenient with his soul in her weaknesses and imperfections and suffer her failings as he suffers those of others, but he must not become idle, and must encourage himself to better things.

Here is a saint, St Seraphim of Sarov, telling me what I cannot be told too often – that I must forgive myself lovingly, as I do others.

AUGUST 29

The man whose silent days
In harmless joys are spent,
Whom hopes cannot delude,
Nor sorrow discontent:
That man needs neither towers
Nor armour for defence,
Nor secret vaults to fly
From thunder's violence.

THOMAS CAMPION

AUGUST 30

People who love themselves but in charity, even as they love their neighbour, bear with themselves charitably (though without flattery) even as one bears with the faults of his neighbour. Such a man exacts not from himself any more than from a neighbour; under the circumstances more than he is capable of bearing; he does not lose heart because he is baffled in his desire to be perfect in a day.

FRANCOIS FENELON

AUGUST 31

I do not find it easy to accept my own feelings. But at the times, anger and pain are natural, as these lines of Alexander Pope say.

Love, hope, and joy, fair pleasure's smiling train,
Hate, fear, and grief, the family of pain,
These mixed with art, and to due bounds confined,
Make and maintain the balance of the mind:
The lights and shades, whose well-accorded strife
Gives all the strength and colour of our life.

SEPTEMBER

SEPTEMBER 1

All things have something more than barren use;
There is a scent upon the briar,
A tremulous splendour in the autumn dews,
Cold morn are fringed with fire.

The clodded earth goes up in sweet-breathed flowers;
In music dies poor human speech,
And into beauty blow those hearts of ours
When Love is born in each.

Daisies are white upon the churchyard sod,
Sweet tears the clouds lean down and give.
The world is very lovely. O my God,
I thank Thee that I live!

All times and all seasons can give us comfort if we have eyes to see the beauty of the world, like the poet Alexander Smith. I have known joy come this way in the midst of inner confusion.

SEPTEMBER 2

So long as there is that which can sin, it is a man. The prayer of misery carries its own justification, when the sober petitions of the self-righteous and the unkind are rejected. He who forgives not is not forgiven, while the cry of a soul out of its fire sets the heartstrings of love trembling.

GEORGE MACDONALD

SEPTEMBER 3

Never give way to melancholy; resist it steadily, for the habit will encroach. I once gave a lady two-and-twenty recipes against melancholy: one was a bright fire; another, to remember all the pleasant things said to and of her; another, to keep a box of sugar-plums on the chimneypiece, and a kettle simmering on the hob.

The nineteenth-century writer Sydney Smith had humour and good sense. I have warded off misery by a strong cup of tea and a slice of homemade cake. Mere trifles can nonetheless comfort us.

SEPTEMBER 4

Thou that hast given so much to me,
Give one thing more, a grateful heart.
See how Thy beggar works on Thee
    By art.
Not thankful, when it pleaseth me;
As if Thy blessings had spare days:
But such a heart, whose pulse may be
    Thy praise.

The cure for self-pity is gratitude. George Herbert's poem points out we can choose to be grateful for the many blessings we have.

SEPTEMBER 5

Calm soul of all things! make it mine
To feel, amid the city's jar,
That there abides a peace of thine,
Man did not make, and cannot mar.

MATTHEW ARNOLD

SEPTEMBER 6

It is no man's business whether he has genius or not: work he must, whatever he is; but quietly and steadily; and the natural and unforced results of such work will be always the things that God meant him to do, and will be his best. No agonies or heart-rendings will enable him to do any better.

Agonizing reduces results, declares John Ruskin. Whether it is a job, work at home or a serious hobby like gardening we do best working with, not against, our own grain.

SEPTEMBER 7

Whither shall I flee from Thy presence?
If I ascend up into heaven, Thou art there: if I make my
bed in hell, behold, Thou art there.
If I take the wings of the morning, and dwell in the
uttermost parts of the sea;
Even there shall Thy hand lead me, and Thy right hand
shall hold me.
If I say, Surely the darkness shall cover me, even the
night shall be light about me.
Yea, the darkness hideth not from Thee.

This inspiring passage about God's relationship with man comes from Psalm 139. I have sometimes felt that God is very far away – only to realise His nearness, most of all when I can't feel His presence.

SEPTEMBER 8

Lovely, lasting peace of mind!
Sweet delight of human kind!
Lovely lasting peace appear!
This world, itself, if thou art here,
Is once again with Eden blessed,
And man contains it in his breast!

THOMAS PARNELL

SEPTEMBER 9

Will you refuse to recognize the divine because it is manifested in art and enjoyment, and not just in conscience and action?

Hippolyte Taine, the French philosopher, shows me that if I see the good only as painful strife, I diminish the good of peace and love. There is a temptation to stress life's struggle rather than to relax into its joys.

SEPTEMBER 10

All Nature is but art, unknown to thee
All chance, direction, which thou canst not see;
All discord, harmony not understood;
All partial evil, universal good.

ALEXANDER POPE

SEPTEMBER 11

Honest gain breeds most joy, I shall add most security, when it is gotten with most pain. Labour is the price we give for after-joys. We look with most delight upon those things which we think to be our own, and we think them most which we have most laboured for.

HENRY VAUGHAN

SEPTEMBER 12

Pleasures lie thickest where no pleasures seem;
There's not a leaf that falls upon the ground
But holds some joy, of silence or of sound,
Some sprite begotten of a summer dream.
The very meanest things are made supreme
With innate ecstasy. No grain of sand
But moves a bright and million-peopled land
And hath its Edens and its Eves, I deem.
For Love, though blind himself, a curious eye
Hath lent me, to behold the hearts of things,
And touched mine ear with power.

Samuel Laman Blanchard was a Victorian poet only a few of whose verses are memorable, including this one. If I look for it I can find the innate ecstasy in the meanest thing around me. I often forget to look.

SEPTEMBER 13

The great pleasure of a dog is that you may make a fool of yourself with him and not only will he not scold you, but he will make a fool of himself too.

As Samuel Butler *says for people with stressful lives, playing with a dog or cat may be a lifeline to joy. Play, like laughter, heals.*

SEPTEMBER 14

And I have felt
A presence that disturbs me with the joy
Of elevated thoughts; a sense sublime
Of something far more deeply interfused,
Whose dwelling is the light of setting suns,
And the round ocean and the living air,
And the blue sky, and in the mind of man;
A motion and a spirit, that impels,
All thinking things, all objects of all thought,
And rolls through all things.

WILLIAM WORDSWORTH

SEPTEMBER 15

Every place I have lived in has its monument of divine love. Every year and every hour of my life has been a time of love. Every friend, every neighbour, and even enemy, have been the messengers and instruments of love. Every state and change of my life, notwithstanding my sin, have opened to me the treasures and mysteries of love.

Minister Richard Baxter saw his many troubles as love.

SEPTEMBER 16

Thus all things ask for rest,
A home above, a home beneath the sod:
The sun will seek the west,
The bird will seek its nest,
The heart another breast
Whereon to lean, the spirit seeks its God.

DORA GREENWELL

SEPTEMBER 17

The greatest mistake you can make in life is to be continually fearing you will makc onc.

ELBERT G. HUBBARD

SEPTEMBER 18

The heart is the capital of the mind;
The mind is a single state;
The heart and mind together make
A single continent.

One is the population –
Numerous enough.
This estatic nation
Seek – it is Yourself.

EMILY DICKINSON

SEPTEMBER 19

It is always the secure who are humble.

G. K. Chesterton is right, of course. Humility is the ability to know myself as I truly am, and to love myself.

SEPTEMBER 20

To escape the distress caused by regret for the past or fear about the future, this is the rule to follow: leave the past to the infinite mercy of God, the future to his good providence; give the present wholly to his love.

JEAN PAUL CAUSSADE

SEPTEMBER 21

Still there is joy that will not cease,
Calm hovering o'er the face of things,
That sweet tranquillity and peace
That morning ever brings.

JOHN CLARE

SEPTEMBER 22

Just as a bicycle chain may be too tight, so may one's carefulness and conscientiousness be so tense as to hinder the running of one's mind.

Too much self-control can do harm, says William James.

SEPTEMBER 23

All is but grief, and heavily we call
On the last terror for the end of all.
Then comes the happy moment: not a stir
In any tree, no portent in the sky:
The morn doth neither hasten nor defer,
The morrow hath no name to call it by,
But life and joy are one – we know not why, –
As though our very blood long breathless lain
Had tasted of the breath of God again.

ROBERT BRIDGES

SEPTEMBER 24

Divine truth is not to be discerned so much in a man's brain, as in his heart.

JOHN SMITH

SEPTEMBER 25

Joy lies close at hand. The dying summer has its own beauty – golden sunlight, late flowers and butterflies. This poem by Mary Russell Mitford describes the inspiration found in her garden.

Within my little garden is a flower,
A tuft of flowers most like a sheaf of corn,
The lilac-blossomed daisy that is born
At Michaelmas, wrought by the gentle power
Of this sweet autumn into one bright shower
Of bloomy beauty. Spring hath nought more fair.
Four sister butterflies inhabit there,
Gay gentle creatures! Round that odorous bower
They weave their dance of joy the livelong day,
Seeming to bless the sunshine; and at night
Fold their enamelled wings as if to pray.
Home-loving pretty ones! would that I might
For richer gifts as cheerful tribute pay,
So meet the rising dawn, so hail the parting ray.

SEPTEMBER 26

The heart is hard in nature, and unfit
For human fellowship, that is not pleased
With sight of animals enjoying life,
Nor feels their happiness augment his own.
The bounding fawn that darts across the glade,
When none pursues, through mere delight of heart,
And spirits buoyant with excess of glee;
The horse as wanton, and almost as fleet,
That skims the spacious meadow at full speed,
Then stops, and snorts, and throwing high his heels
Starts to the voluntary race again.

These lines are by William Cowper, the tender-hearted poet who struggled against depression all his life, finding comfort and joy in his pet hares and birds, and in the wild animals around him.

SEPTEMBER 27

When the sun rises, do you not see a round disk of fire somewhat like a guinea? O no, no! I see an innumerable company of the heavenly host crying 'Holy, holy, holy, is the Lord God Almighty.'

WILLIAM BLAKE

SEPTEMBER 28

There is a time to be idle, as well as a time to work, which is why I like this poem by the American doctor S. Weir Mitchell.

There is no dearer lover of lost hours
Than I.
I can be idler than the idlest flowers;
More idly lie
Than noonday lilies languidly afloat
And water pillowed in a windless moat.
And I can be
Stiller than some gray stone
That hath no motion known.
It seems to me
That my still idleness doth make my own
All magic gifts of joy's simplicity.

SEPTEMBER 29

In the meantime we are born only to be men. We shall do enough if we form ourselves to be good ones. It is therefore our business carefully to cultivate in our minds every sort of generous and honest feeling that belongs to our nature.

Good advice from the eighteenth-century thinker Edmund Burke. We can only work within human limits.

SEPTEMBER 30

God give thee
Time for the task,
Wisdom for the work,
Grace for the way,
Love to the last.

ANONYMOUS

OCTOBER

OCTOBER 1

The autumn time has come;
On woods that dream of bloom,
And over purpling vines,
The low sun fainter shines.

The aster flower is failing,
The hazel's gold is paling;
Yet overhead more near
The eternal stars appear.

And present gratitude
Insures the future's good,
And for the things I see
I trust the things to be;

That in the paths untrod,
And the long days of God,
My feet shall still be led,
My heart be comforted.

JOHN GREENLEAF WHITTIER

OCTOBER 2

No one is useless in the world who lightens the burden of it for anyone else.

CHARLES DICKENS

OCTOBER 3

And this for comfort thou must
know:
Times that are ill won't still be so;
Clouds will not ever pour down
rain;
A sullen day will clear again.

In times of trouble, the most comforting thought I can have is that trouble will not last for ever – as Robert Herrick says.

OCTOBER 4

It is a strange fact but you can often handle two difficulties – your own and somebody else's – better than you can handle your own alone. That truth is based on the subtle law of self-giving or outgoingness whereby you develop a self-strengthening in the process. If you have a tough difficulty, look around until you find somebody who has a worse difficulty than yours, then start helping that individual. You will find in so doing that your own problem, when finally you have helped the other person with his, will be much simpler, much clearer, much easier to handle.

Helping others, as Norman Vincent Peale says, certainly seems to take my mind off its own troubles and thus relieve them.

OCTOBER 5

Joy is not in things: it is in us.

RICHARD WAGNER

OCTOBER 6

On the whole, we are meant to look after ourselves; it
is certain
Each has to eat for himself, digest for himself, and in
general
Care for his own dear life, and see to his own
preservation;
Nature's intentions, in most things uncertain, in this
are decisive.

When I fail to love, care for and look after myself, as I sometimes do, I am going against what is natural, says Arthur Hugh Clough.

OCTOBER 7

The day returns and brings us the petty round of irritating concerns and duties. Help us to perform them with laughter and kind faces. Let cheerfulness abound with industry. Give us strength to go blithely on our business all this day. Bring us to our resting beds weary and content and undishonoured; and grant us in the end the gift of sleep.

This prayer was written by Robert Louis Stevenson.

OCTOBER 8

Do not fear to hope ...
Each time we smell the autumn's dying scent,
We know that primrose time will come again.

SAMUEL TAYLOR COLERIDGE

OCTOBER 9

O world, thou choosest not the better part!
It is not wisdom to be only wise,
And on the inward vision close the eyes,
But it is wisdom to believe the heart.

GEORGE SANTAYANA

OCTOBER 10

Let us spend one day as deliberately as nature, and not be thrown off the track by every nutshell and mosquito's wing that falls on the rails. Let us rise early and fast, or break fast, gently and without perturbation; let company come and let company go, let the bells ring and the children cry – determined to make a day of it. If the engine whistles, let it whistle till it is hoarse for its pains. If the bell rings, why should we run? Time is but the stream I go a-fishing in.

I fight rather than accept circumstances, trying to do too much. Henry David Thoreau, the American essayist, has a lesson for me.

OCTOBER 11

Give, dear O Lord,
Fine weather in its day,
Plenty on the board,
And a good heart all the way.

CONSTANCE HOLME

OCTOBER 12

Go out into the woods and valleys, when your heart is rather harassed than bruised, and when you suffer from vexation more than grief. Then the trees all hold out their arms to you to relieve you of the burthen of your heavy thoughts; and the streams under the trees glance at you as they run by, and will carry away your trouble along with the fallen leaves.

ROBERT VAUGHAN

It is the greatest of all mistakes to do nothing because you can only do little. OCTOBER 13

SYDNEY SMITH

These two verses from a poem by Francis Thompson are yet another call to find the spiritual in the ordinary. Great powers, like unseen angels, are all around us: ours to sense if we choose. OCTOBER 14

Not where the wheeling systems darken
And our benumbed conceiving soars! –
The drift of pinions, would we hearken,
Beats at our own clay-shuttered doors.

The angels keep their ancient places; –
Turn but a stone and start a wing!
'Tis ye, 'tis your estrangèd faces
That miss the many-splendoured thing.

OCTOBER 15

Who knows not friendship, knows not bliss sincere.
Court it, ye young; ye aged, bind it fast;
Earn it, ye proud; nor think the purchase dear,
Whate'er the labour if 'tis gained at last.

These rather formal lines about friendship were written two centuries ago by William Whitehead. Let us not undervalue the powers of friendship to make life happier. We need our friends.

OCTOBER 16

Be not anxious for your life, what ye shall eat, or what ye shall drink; not yet for your body, what ye shall put on. Is not the life more than the food, and the body more than the raiment? Behold the birds of heaven, that they sow not, neither do they reap, nor gather into barns; and your heavenly Father feedeth them. Are not ye of much more value than they? And which of you by being anxious can add one cubit unto his statue? Be not therefore anxious for the morrow, for the morrow will be anxious for itself.

These familiar words are from Jesus of Nazareth. Most of my anxieties, which seem so real, are unnecessary: I must try not to waste time and energy even giving them space in my head.

OCTOBER 17

Hold thou my hands!
In grief and joy, in hope and fear,
Lord, let me feel that Thou art near:
Hold thou my hands!

WILLIAM CANTON

OCTOBER 18

Lord, temper with tranquillity our manifold activity, that we may do our work for Thee with very great simplicity.

I found this on a card in a country church. I must cultivate the inner calm which will prevent me from complicating my life.

OCTOBER 19

Love to faults is always blind
Always is to joy inclined,
Lawless, winged, and unconfined,
And breaks all chains from every mind.

WILLIAM BLAKE

OCTOBER 20

Peace comes when we have learned to accept, not so much with resignation as with a dutiful response to reality, the evil we confront as part of our nature. We no longer hate ourselves for being what we are; we no longer blaspheme because we have been created just so and not otherwise; we are no longer in revolt, with an insolent egoism, against our own imperfection. We are content, in a word, to be men and not God.

VICTOR GOLLANCZ

OCTOBER 21

'Tis being and doing and having that make
All the pleasures and pains of which mankind partake;
To be what God pleases, to do a man's best,
And to have a good heart, is the way to be blest.

GEORGE LORD BYRON

OCTOBER 22

This visible world is wonderfully to be delighted in and highly to be esteemed because it is the theatre of God's righteous kingdom. No man can sin that clearly seeth the beauty of God's face, because no man can sin against his own happiness. By faith therefore we are to live and sharpen our eye that we may see His glory.

THOMAS TRAHERNE

OCTOBER 23

Though nothing can bring back the hour
Of splendour in the grass, of glory in the flower;
We will grieve not, rather find
Strength in what remains behind,
In the primal sympathy
Which having been must ever be,
In the soothing thoughts that spring
Out of human suffering.

WILLIAM WORDSWORTH

OCTOBER 24

When men are rightly occupied, then amusement grows out of the work as the colour-petals out of a fruitful flower; when they are faithfully helpful and compassionate, all their emotions become steady, deep, perpetual and vivifying to the soul as the natural pulse to the body.

JOHN RUSKIN

OCTOBER 25

Growth begins when we start to accept our own weakness.

JEAN VANIER

OCTOBER 26

Domestic happiness, thou only bliss
Of Paradise, that hast survived the fall!
Thou art the nurse of Virtue; in thine arms
She smiles, appearing, as in truth she is,
Heaven born, and destined to the skies again.
Thou art not known where pleasure is adored,
For thou art meek and constant, hating change,
And finding in the calm of truth-tried love
Joys that her stormy raptures never yield.

I don't know why poets have so often neglected the obvious – that most of our happiness comes from a happy home. William Cowper, who wrote these lines, lived quietly in the country for many years with the comfort of friends, pets, and a garden.

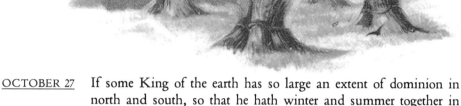

OCTOBER 27

If some King of the earth has so large an extent of dominion in north and south, so that he hath winter and summer together in his dominions, so large an extent east and west, as that he hath day and night together in his dominions, much more hath God mercy and judgement together. God comes to thee, not as in the dawning of the day, not as in the bud of the spring, but as the sun at noon to illustrate all shadows, as the sheaves in harvest to fill all penuries. All occasions invite his mercies and all times are his seasons.

This extract from a sermon by John Donne is about the generosity of God, a generosity beyond our imagination. The passage is favourite of Maria Browne, and is here to mark her birthday.

OCTOBER 28

Without winter, there can be no spring.
Without mistakes, there can be no learning.
Without doubts, there can be no faith.
Without fears, there can be no courage.
My mistakes, my fears and my doubts are my path to
wisdom, faith and courage.

AUTHOR UNKNOWN

OCTOBER 29

This is the prayer of Abu Bakr, the father in law of the prophet Mohammed. It is quite a subtle prayer and takes a little working out. It's better than just clever: it's accurate about human nature!

I thank Thee, Lord, for knowing
me better than I know myself,
And for letting me know myself
better than others know me.
I pray Thee then, make me better
than they suppose,
And forgive me for what they
do not know.

OCTOBER 30

Happiness, like virtue, is acquired by practice.

ANONYMOUS

OCTOBER 31

When the dumb hour, clothed in black,
Brings the dreams about my bed,
Call me not so often back,
Silent voices of the dead,
Toward the lowland ways behind me,
And the sunlight that is gone!
Call me rather, silent voices,
Forward to the starry track
Glimmering up the heights beyond me
On, and always on.

On All Souls' Night, this poem remembers friends who have died. Alfred, Lord Tennyson, who lost his best friend, says we should use memories of those who have died as an inspiration for the future.

NOVEMBER

NOVEMBER 1

To you the beauties of the autumnal year
Make mournful emblems, and you think of man
Doomed to the grave's long winter, spirit broke,
Sense-dulled and fretful. To me they show
The calm decay of nature, when the mind
Retains its strength, and in the languid eye
Religion's holy hopes kindle a joy
That makes old age look lovely. Oh, my friend,
That thy faith were as mine! that thou couldst see
Death still producing life, and evil still
Working its own destruction; couldst behold
The strifes and tumults of this troubled world
With the strong eye that sees the promised day
Dawn through this night of tempest! All things then
Would minister to joy; then should thine heart
Be healed and harmonized and thou shouldst feel
God, always, everywhere, and all in all.

ROBERT SOUTHEY

NOVEMBER 2

Laughter has something in it in common with the ancient winds of faith and inspiration; it unfreezes pride and unwinds secrecy; it makes men forget themselves in the presence of something greater than themselves; something that they cannot resist.

G.K. CHESTERTON

NOVEMBER

NOVEMBER 3

That the birds of worry and care fly above your head, this you cannot change. But that they build nests in your hair, this you can prevent.

CHINESE PROVERB

NOVEMBER 4

The sea awoke at midnight from its sleep,
And round the pebbly beaches far and wide
I heard the first wave of the rising tide
Rush onward with uninterrupted sweep;
A voice out of the silence of the deep,
A sound mysteriously multiplied
As of a cataract from the mountain's side,
Or roar of winds upon a wooded steep.
So comes to us at times, from the unknown
And inaccessible solitudes of being,
The rushing of the sea-tides of the soul;
And inspirations, that we deem our own,
Are some divine foreshadowing and foreseeing
Of things beyond our reason or control.

HENRY WADSWORTH LONGFELLOW

NOVEMBER 5

The real animating power of knowledge is only in the moment of its being first received, when it fills us with wonder and joy; a joy for which, observe, the previous ignorance is just as necessary as the present knowledge.

John Ruskin recognizes the joy of learning something new.

NOVEMBER 6

No man e'er found a happy life by chance,
Or yawned it into being with a wish.
An art it is, and must be learnt; and learnt
With unremitting effort, or be lost.

EDWARD YOUNG

NOVEMBER 7

We can find joy and inspiration in other species. Here is the prayer of a dog. The author is Piero Scanziani. I love his idea.

O Lord of all creatures, make the man my master, as faithful to other men as I am to him. Make him as loving to his family and friends as I am to him. Give him, O Lord, an easy and spontaneous smile, easy and spontaneous as when I wag my tail. May he be as readily grateful, as I am quick to lick his hand. Grant him patience equal to mine, when I await his return without complaining. Give him my courage, my readiness to sacrifice everything for him in all circumstances, even life itself. Keep for him the youthfulness of my heart and the cheerfulness of my thoughts. O Lord of all creatures, as I am always truly a dog, grant that he may be always truly a man.

NOVEMBER 8

I go to prove my soul!
I shall arrive! what time, what circuit first,
I ask not; but unless God send his hail
Or blinding fireballs, sleet or stifling snow,
In some good time, His good time, I shall arrive;
He guides me and the bird. In His good time!

ROBERT BROWNING

NOVEMBER 9

Man can see his reflection only when he bends down close to it; and the heart of man, too, must lean down to the heart of his fellow; then it will see itself within his heart.

JEWISH HASIDIC SAYING

NOVEMBER 10

I have said that the soul is not more than the body,
And I have said that the body is not more than the soul,
And nothing, not God, is greater to one than one's self is,
And I say to any man or women, Let your soul stand
    cool and composed before a million universes.

WALT WHITMAN

NOVEMBER 11

Hast thou not seen how all in the heavens and in the earth uttereth the praise of God – the very birds as they spread their wings? Every creature knoweth its prayer and its praise. And God knoweth what they do.

THE KORAN

NOVEMBER 12

In a thousand senses, true work is worship. He that works, whatever be his work, he bodies forth the form of things unseen; a small poet every worker is.

THOMAS CARLYLE

NOVEMBER 13

And can He who smiles on all
Hear the wren with sorrow small,
Hear the small bird's grief and care,
Hear the woes that infants bear –

And not sit beside the nest,
Pouring pity in their breast,
And not sit the cradle near
Weeping tear on infant's tear?

Thinkst not thou canst sigh a sigh,
And thy Maker is not by:
Think not thou canst weep a tear
And thy Maker is not near.

WILLIAM BLAKE

NOVEMBER 14

'Twill all be well: no need of care;
Though how it will, and when or where,
We cannot see, and can't declare.
In spite of dreams, in spite of thought,
'Tis not in vain and not for nought
The wind it blows, the ship it goes,
Though where and whither no one knows.

ARTHUR HUGH CLOUGH

NOVEMBER 15

I should learn to co-operate, quietly and in complete freedom, with His blessed and blessing will, that will of His which I discover deep in my own heart as my own will also – as the best essential me – and which, discovering it also deep in the heart of everything else, I find to be not only vaster, but also saner and more fruitful of life and peace and joy, than the self-regarding wilfulness that would deceive me with its appearance of leading me to my goal, but would in fact cut me off, if it had its way, from my birthright of unity with all things.

VICTOR GOLLANCZ

NOVEMBER 16

Perhaps the most deceptively simple but subtle prayer of all is this one from the followers of Mani, a third-century prophet.

Do Thou in me make peace, O light-bringer.

NOVEMBER 17

How happy is the little stone
That rambles in the road alone,
And doesn't care about careers
And exigencies never fears;
Whose coat of elemental brown
A passing universe put on,
And independent as the sun
Associates or glows alone;
Fulfilling absolute decree
In casual simplicity.

EMILY DICKINSON

NOVEMBER 18

When one sees the tree in leaf, one thinks the beauty of the tree is in its leaves, and then one sees the bare tree.

Samuel Menaste starts his poetry sequence, 'The Bay Tree', with this quotation by Sarah Brana Barak. It is not just about trees.

NOVEMBER 19

And let the counsel of thine own heart stand; for there is no man more faithful unto thee than it.
For a man's mind is sometimes wont to tell him more than seven watchmen, that sit above in a high tower.

Have faith in your self, say these verses from Ecclesiastes.

NOVEMBER 20

All sorrow and all joy come from love.

The medieval German mystic, Meister Eckehart points out that we cannot have the joys of love and friendship without their sorrows too.

NOVEMBER 21

All are but parts of one stupendous whole,
Whose body nature is, and God the soul;
That, changed through all, and yet in all the same;
Great in the earth, as in the ethereal frame;
Warms in the sun, refreshes in the breeze,
Glows in the stars, and blossoms in the trees;
Lives through all life, extends through all extent;
Spreads undivided, operates unspent!

ALEXANDER POPE

NOVEMBER 22

All musical people seem to me happy; it is the most engrossing pursuit; almost the only innocent and unpunished passion.

Today is dedicated to St Cecilia, the patron saint of music. Sydney Smith's words remind me of the simple joy of listening to music.

NOVEMBER 23

In that hour
From out my sullen heart a power
Broke like a rainbow from the shower,
To feel, although no tongue can prove,
That every cloud that spreads above
And veileth love, itself is love.

ALFRED, LORD TENNYSON

NOVEMBER 24

Nor can we fall below the arms of God, how low soever it be we fall.

Anger, depression, indeed all human sin and suffering only elicit more of God's love, says the Quaker writer William Penn.

NOVEMBER 25

All that matters is to be at one with the living God
To be a creature in the house of the God of life.

Like a cat asleep in a chair
At peace, in peace
And at one with the master of the house, with the
mistress,
At home, at home in the house of the living,
Sleeping on the hearth, and yawning before the fire.

Sleeping on the hearth of the living world
Yawning at home before the fire of life
Feeling the presence of the living God
Like a great reassurance
A deep calm in the heart.

DAVID HERBERT LAWRENCE

NOVEMBER 26

Sybil of months and worshipper of winds
I love thee, rude and boisterous as thou art.
And scraps of joy my wandering ever finds
'Mid thy uproarious madness – when the start
Of sudden tempests stir the forest leaves
Into hoarse fury, till the shower set free
Still the huge swells and ebb the mighty heaves
That swing the forest like a troubled sea.
I love the wizard noise, and rave in turn
Half vacant thoughts and self-imagined rhymes.

NOVEMBER 27 *Like the nature poet, John Clare, I can find a freedom and an excitement in bad weather. November winds elate me, set me free from small obsessions and remind me of greater powers.*

Worry means always and invariably loss of effective power. Of course, the sovereign cure for worry is faith. To him who has a hold on vaster and more permanent realities, the hourly vicissitudes of his personal destiny seem relatively insignificant things.

WILLIAM JAMES

NOVEMBER 28

O where Thy voice doth come
Let all doubts be dumb,
Let all words be mild,
All strifes be reconciled,
All pains beguiled!
Light bring no blindness,
Love no unkindness,
Knowledge no ruin,
Fear no undoing!

MATTHEW ARNOLD

NOVEMBER 29

That man who does not believe that each day contains an earlier, more sacred and auroral hour than any he has yet profaned, has despaired of life, and is pursuing a descending and darkening way.

To take a day for granted is to extinguish all possibility of joy, says Henry David Thoreau. Each new day brings new possibilities of love, beauty and happiness.

NOVEMBER 30

Talk not of sad November, when a day
Of warm, glad sunshine fills the sky of noon,
And a wind, borrowed from some morn of June,
Stirs the brown grasses and the leafless spray.

Close to my heart I fold each lovely thing
The sweet day yields; and, not disconsolate,
With the calm patience of the woods I wait
For leaf and blossom when God gives us spring.

JOHN GREENLEAF WHITTIER

DECEMBER

DECEMBER 1

How still, how happy! Now I feel
Where silence dwells is sweeter far
Than laughing mirth's most joyous swell,
However pure its raptures are.

Come, sit down on this sunny stone:
'Tis wintry light o'er flowerless moors –
But sit – for we are all alone,
And clear expand heaven's breathless shores.

Yet my heart loves December's smile
As much as July's golden beam;
Then let us sit and watch the while
The blue ice curdling on the stream.

There is a special, remarkable quietness outdoors in the really cold weather, which the writer Emily Brontë found inspiring.

DECEMBER 2

Imagine a man whose business hounds him the livelong day. Only when the time for the afternoon prayer comes, does he remember 'I must pray'. Then from the bottom of his heart he heaves a sigh of regret that he has spent his day on vain and idle matters, and he runs into a by-street and stands there and prays. God holds him dear, very dear, and his prayer pierces the firmament.

BAAL SHEM TOV

DECEMBER 3

O never star
Was lost; here
We all aspire to heaven and there is heaven
Above us.
If I stoop
Into a dark tremendous sea of cloud,
It is but for a time; I press God's lamp
Close to my breast; its splendour soon or late
Will pierce the gloom. I shall emerge some day.

ROBERT BROWNING

DECEMBER 4

Of what is valuable and excellent, the gods grant nothing to mankind without labour and care; if you seek to be beloved by your friends, you must serve your friends; if you desire to be honoured by any city, you must benefit that city; or if you wish to be vigorous in body, you must accustom your body to obey your mind, and exercise it with toil and exertion.

Ancient Greek philosopher Socrates explains that there is no easy to way to achievement. A modern saying is 'No gain without pain.'

DECEMBER 5

We shun it ere it comes,
Afraid of joy,
Then sue it to delay
And lest it fly,
Beguile it more and more –
May not this be
Old suitor heaven,
Like our dismay at thee?

I find this poem by Emily Dickinson very perceptive. If I am not aware, I can deny the joy within. It needs my turning away from my cares, to let it flower. Nor must I try to hold on to it too long.

DECEMBER 6

Success is to be measured not so much by the position one has reached in life, as by the obstacles which he has overcome while trying to succeed.

BOOKER T. WASHINGTON

DECEMBER 7

Seek love in the pity of others' woe,
In the gentle relief of another's care,
In the darkness of night and the winter's snow,
In the naked and outcast, seek love there.

WILLIAM BLAKE

DECEMBER 8

Be not righteous over much, neither make thy self over wise, lest thou destroy thyself.

For those like myself who tend to be over-serious, this is good advice from Ecclesiastes. We all need to be childish, even foolish at times.

DECEMBER 9

Our highest truths are but half-truths.
Think not to settle down forever in any truth.
Make use of it as a tent in which to pass a summer's night,
But build not house of it, or it will be your tomb.
When you first have an inkling of its insufficiency,
And begin to descry a dim counter-truth looming up beyond,
Then weep not, but give thanks,
It is the Lord's voice whispering: 'Take up thy bed and walk.'

ARTHUR JAMES BALFOUR

DECEMBER 10

The best way out of emotional pain is through it.

AUTHOR UNKNOWN

DECEMBER 11

One of the best ways to tackle a difficult task is to think of the least thing you can do towards the task, and do that. Thousands of years ago the Chinese Tao philosopher, Lao Tzu, put it this way.

Manage the difficult while they are easy.
Manage the great while they are small.
All difficult things in the world start from the easy;
All great things in the world start from the small.
The tree that fills a man's arms arises from a tender shoot.
The nine-storeyed tower is raised from a heap of earth;
A thousand miles' journey begins from the spot under one's feet.

DECEMBER 12

In seeking wisdom, the first step is silence, the second listening, the third remembering, the fourth practising, the fifth – teaching others.

IBN GABIROL

DECEMBER 13

It is a sweet thing, friendship, a dear balm,
A happy and auspicious bird of calm,
Which rides o'er life's ever tumultuous ocean;
A god that broods o'er chaos in commotion;
A flower which fresh as Lapland roses are,
Lifts its bold head into the world's frore air,
And blooms most radiantly when others die,
Health, hope, and youth, and brief prosperity;
... a star
Which moves not 'mid the moving heavens
alone –
A smile among dark frowns – a gentle
tone
Among rude voices, a belovèd light,
A solitude, a refuge, a delight.

This lovely passage about the joy of friendship by Percy Bysshe Shelley comes naturally at this time when Christmas approaches.

DECEMBER 14

In rigorous hours, when down the iron lane
The redbreast looks in vain
For hips and haws,
Lo, shining flowers upon my window-pane
The silver pencil of the winter draws.

When all the snowy hill
And the bare woods are still;
When snipes are silent in the frozen bogs,
And all the garden garth is whelmed in mire,
Lo, by the hearth, the laughter of the logs –
More fair than roses, lo, the flowers of fire!

One of the simple joys of winter is an open fire. This poem by Robert Louis Stevenson is about the cheerfulness of the hearth.

DECEMBER 15

Crossing a bare common, in snow puddles, at twilight, under a clouded sky, without having in my thoughts any occurrence of special good fortune, I have enjoyed a perfect exhilaration. I am glad to the brink of fear.

RALPH WALDO EMERSON

DECEMBER 16

Don't be too severe upon yourself and your own failings; keep on, don't faint, be energetic to the last.

REV. SYDNEY SMITH

DECEMBER 17

The world has no such flowers in any land
And no such pearl in any gulf the sea
As any babe on any mother's knee.

ALGERNON CHARLES SWINBURNE

DECEMBER 18

O Lord! Thou knowest how busy I must be this day: if I forget thee, do not Thou forget me.

This is the prayer uttered by Sir Philip Warwick before the Battle of Edgehill. I use it in the busy days before Christmas.

DECEMBER 19

Life is so generous a giver, but we, judging its gifts by
their covering, cast them away as ugly or heavy or hard.
Remove the covering, and you will find beneath it a living
splendour, woven of love, by wisdom with power.
Welcome it, grasp it, and you touch the angel's hand that
brings it to you.
Everything that we call a trial, a sorrow, or a duty,
Believe me that the angel's hand is there; the gift is there,
and the wonder of an overshadowing presence.
Our joys too: be not content with them as joys.
They too conceal diviner gifts.

FRA GIOVANNI

DECEMBER 20 *This poem by William Canton is titled 'In Praise of Children'.*

The earth which feels the flowering of a thorn,
Was glad, O little child, when you were born.
The earth, which thrills when skylarks scale the blue,
Soared up itself to God's own heaven in you.
And heaven, which loves to lean down and to glass
Its beauty in each dewdrop on the grass –
Heaven laughed to find your face so pure and fair,
And left, O little child, its reflex there.

DECEMBER 21 Are you willing to forget what you have done for other people, and to remember what other people have done for you; to ignore what the world owes you, and to think what you owe the world; to put your rights in the background and your duties in the middle distance and your chances to do a little more than your duty in the foreground; to see that your fellow men are just as real as you are, and to try to look behind their faces to their hearts hungry for joy? Then you can keep Christmas.

HENRY VAN DYKE

DECEMBER 22

Now Christmas is come,
Let us beat up the drum,
And call all our neighbours together;
And when they appear,
Let us make them such cheer
As will keep out the wind and the weather.

AUTHOR UNKNOWN

DECEMBER 23

There is something in the very season of the year that gives a charm to the festivity of Christmas. In the depth of winter, when nature lies despoiled of every charm and wrapped in her shroud of sheeted snow, we turn for our gratifications to moral sources. We feel more sensibly the charm of each other's society, and are brought more closely together by dependence on each other for enjoyment. Heart calleth to heart; and we draw our pleasures from the deep wells of living kindness, which lie in the quiet recesses of our bosoms. Where does the honest face of hospitality expand into a broader and more cordial smile than by the winter fireside? Amid the general call to happiness, the bustle of the spirits, and stir of affections, which prevail at this period, what bosom can remain insensible? It is, indeed, the season of regenerated feeling – the season for kindling not merely the fire of hospitality in the hall, but the genial flame of charity in the heart.

WASHINGTON IRVING

DECEMBER 24

Christmas Eve, and twelve of the clock.
'Now they are all on their knees,'
An elder said as we sat in a flock
By the embers in hearthside ease.

We pictured the meek mild creatures where
They dwelt in their strawy pen,
Nor did it occur to one of us there
To doubt they were kneeling then.

So fair a fancy few would weave
In these years! Yet, I feel,
If someone said on Christmas Eve,
'Come; see the oxen kneel

'In the lonely barton by yonder coomb
Our childhood used to know,'
I should go with him in the gloom,
Hoping it might be so.

THOMAS HARDY

DECEMBER 25

And there were in the same country, shepherds abiding in the field, keeping watch over their flock by night,

And, lo, the angel of the Lord came upon them, and the glory of the Lord shone round about them: and they were sore afraid.

And the angel said unto them, Fear not: for, behold, I bring you good tidings of great joy, which shall be to all people.

For unto you is born this day in the city of David a Saviour, which is Christ the Lord.

And this shall be a sign unto you; Ye shall find the babe wrapped in swaddling clothes, lying in a manger.

GOSPEL OF ST LUKE

DECEMBER 26

Where is this stupendous stranger,
Swains of Solyma, advise,
Lead me to my Master's manager,
Shew me where my Saviour lies?

Nature's decorations glisten
Far above their usual trim;
Birds on box and laurel listen,
As so near the cherubs hymn.

God all-bounteous, all-creative,
Whom no ills from good dissuade,
Is incarnate, and a native
Of the very world he made.

CHRISTOPHER SMART

DECEMBER 27

May each Christmas, as it comes, find us more and more like Him who at this time became a little child, for our sake; more simple-minded, more humble, more affectionate, more resigned, more happy, more full of God.

These words of Cardinal John Newman remind me that there is a child within us. Encouraging that child within leads to happiness.

DECEMBER 28

O perfect Love, outpassing sight,
O Light beyond our ken,
Come down through all the world tonight,
And heal the hearts of men.

LAURENCE HOUSMAN

DECEMBER 29

Nearer and closer to our hearts be the Christmas spirit, which is the spirit of active usefulness, perseverance, cheerful discharge of duty, kindness and forbearance.

CHARLES DICKENS

DECEMBER 30

The writer Charles Lamb had a talent for finding enjoyment where he could, despite money worries and constant care for his ill sister. He lists the pleasures that are available to nearly all of us.

Sun, and sky, and breeze, and solitary walks, and summer holidays, and the greenness of fields, and the delicious juices of meats and fishes, and society, and the cheerful glass, and candle-light, and fireside conversations and innocent vanities and jests.

DECEMBER 31

Almost everybody knows this beautiful passage from St Paul's letter to the Corinthians. I certainly do. Yet each time I read it I can find comfort and joy in reminding myself of the nature of love. It applies to the way I should treat my family, my friends, the people I work with, those strangers I encounter during my day. It also applies to the way I should treat myself, being patient with myself, forgiving myself and caring for myself. I will take these words for the end of this year and the start of the new one.

Love suffereth long, and is kind; love envieth not; love
vaunteth not itself, is not puffed up,
Doth not behave itself unseemly, seeketh not its own,
is not provoked, taketh not account of evil;
Rejoiceth not in unrighteousness, but rejoiceth with
the truth;
Beareth all things, believeth all things, hopeth all things,
endureth all things.
But now abideth faith, hope, love, these three; and the
greatest of these is love.
Follow after love.

ACKNOWLEDGEMENTS

I have tried to obtain permission from copyright holders to reproduce the quotations in this book, but there are some I could not trace. The publishers will be happy to rectify any omissions in future editions. I should like to thank the following for permission to reprint extracts:

The Earl of Balfour for a poem by Arthur James Balfour.

Gerard Benson for 'Glendalough', first published in *Ore* magazine.

The Buddhist Society for an extract from 'Tao Te Ching' by Lao Tzu, translated by Ch'u Ta-Kao, published by the Buddhist Lodge, 1937.

Collins for extracts from *A Gift from God*, by Mother Teresa of Calcutta.

Faber and Faber Ltd for extracts from *Diary of a Russian Priest* by Alexander Elchaninov.

Peters Fraser and Dunlop Group Ltd for 'Courtesy' by Hilaire Belloc, in *Sonnets and Verse*, Gerald Duckworth and Co. Ltd.

Victor Gollancz Ltd for extracts from *From Darkness to Light* by Victor Gollancz.

Gordon Press, New York, for permission to quote from the works of Elbert G. Hubbard.

Harper and Row Inc., New York, for extracts from *The Autobiography of Eleanor Roosevelt*, by Anna Eleanor Roosevelt.

David Higham Associates for extracts from *The Book of Comfort*, by Elizabeth Goudge, Michael Joseph.

Hodder and Stoughton Ltd and Richard Scott Simon Ltd for an extract from *Bolts from the Blue*, copyright © 1986 by Rabbi Lionel Blue, Hodder and Stoughton Ltd.

The Literary Trustees of Walter de la Mare and the Society of Authors as their representative for 'Courage' by Walter de la Mare.

Jess McAree for his translation of Francis Jammes' poem.

Samuel Menashe for permission to quote from his poetry sequence, 'The Bare Tree' from *Collected Poems*, published by the National Poetry Foundation, the University of Maine, Orono, Maine.

Methuen London Ltd for permission to quote William Inge.

The MIT Press for an extract from *Faith* by George Santayana.

John Murray (Publishers) Ltd for an extract from *The Story of San Michele* by Axel Munthe.

The Octogan Press Ltd for an extract from Al-Ghazzali's *The Alchemy of Happiness*, published by the Octagon Press Ltd (1980).

Oxford University Press for 'A Song of Good Heart' by Constance Holme, and 'The Maker of the Sun and Moon' by Laurence Housman, from the *English Hymnal*.

Laurence Pollinger Ltd and the estate of Frieda Laurence Ravagli for 'Pax' from *The Complete Poems of D.H. Lawrence*, Copyright © 1964, 1971 by Angelo Ravagli and C. M. Weekley, executors of the Estate of Frieda Laurence Ravagli. Used by permission of Viking Penguin, a division of Penguin USA.

Prentice-Hall, Inc., Englewood Cliffs, New Jersey, for extracts from *The Positive Principle Today* by Norman Vincent Peale, 1976.

Random House Inc. for an extract from *Tales of the Hasidim: The Early Masters/The Later Masters*, by Martin Buber, translated by Olga Marx, Copyright © 1947, 1948 and renewed 1975 by Schocken Books Inc. Reprinted by permission of Schocken Books, published by Pantheon Books, a division of Random House, Inc.

SCM Press and Macmillan Publishing Co, New York, for 'Morning Prayers' from *Letters and Papers from Prison*, by Dietrich Bonhoeffer, the Enlarged Edition, © SCM Press 1971.

Sidgwick and Jackson Ltd for 'Ducks' by F.W. Harvey.

The Society of Authors on behalf of the Bernard Shaw Estate for an extract from 'The Revolutionist's Handbook' in *Man and Superman*.

PICTURE CREDITS

January: Joseph Farquarson, *Glowed with Tints of Evening Hours* (Bridgeman Art Library/Roy Miles); February: William B. Fortescue, *February* (Bridgeman); March: Joseph Kirkpatrick, *The Lost Lamb* (Priory Gallery); April: Edward Wilkins Waite, *Near Brockham, Surrey* (Bridgeman); May: Helen Allingham, *Bluebells* (Bridgeman); June: Joyce Haddon, *Beehive with Doves*; July: Helen Allingham, *Summer Flowers* (Bridgeman); August: Myles Birket Foster, *Cullercoats* (Bridgeman); September: Frederick Morgan, *The Apple Gatherers* (Bridgeman); October: Edward W. Waite, *A Country Road in Autumn* (Bridgeman); November: Frederick Daniel Hardy, *The Convalescent* (Bridgeman); December: Albert Chevalier Tayler, *The Christmas Tree* (Bridgeman).